About this book

Hinduism, Spirituality and the Misconceptions was written with the intention of helping people who do not truly understand aspects of spirituality or Hinduism. I once had many questions with barely any answers. After years of searching high and low, I finally began to obtain some of the answers I had been looking for.

With so many different views, sects and religious leaders, who do you really listen to in order to get your answers? Some have conflicting views, so what do you take to be true? In my personal experience, this is one of the many issues that has really confused me and threw me off balance.

Eventually, at a later stage in my life, I had met my guru, Maldev Bapa. I obtained a lot of my knowledge through my guru. There is a lineage of 700 years' worth of knowledge that my guru has passed on to me. One of his predecessors was the renowned Kabir Sahib. The lineage is as follows: Ramanand Sahib, Kabir Sahib, Bhan Sahib, Ravi Sahib, Ugmeshwar Sahib, Labheshwar Nath, Hathya Sahib, and Maldev Bapa.

I hope this book answers some, if not all, of your questions, guides you and satisfies you in the way my thirst for truth and knowledge was satisfied. In all honesty, as long as I help one person in the world through this book and the knowledge within it, I am content.

The layout

This book is set out in a question and answer format in order to provide you with a complete learning experience. The book focuses on the most common questions people have.

There is a glossary towards the back of the book to assist the reader with unfamiliar terminology.

What can you take away from this book?

The readers of this book will have varying levels of understanding of Hinduism and spirituality. The advice of the author is to understand the context of the examples given and take the points they feel are relevant to them.

Dedication

I dedicate this book to my guru, Maldev Bapa, for all that he has taught me. I hope the knowledge within this book assists others on their path of Hinduism and spirituality.

Acknowledgements

I would like to thank my editor for their hard work and dedication towards this book, without whom publishing this book would not be possible.

I would like to thank Madhav Gohil and Prafula Gohil for the initial proofreading and assisting in the creation of parts of the content.

I would like to thank Parita Kansara, Kavita Mardania, Divya Mardania and Kushna Shah for completing the final proof read of the book.

Chapter 1- Hinduism 101

What is Hinduism?

The term Hindu was given by foreigners to people living by the River Indu, sometimes called the River Sindhu. This is why the world now knows the religion as Hinduism. The true name for what we call modern day Hinduism is Sanathan Dharma. Sanathan means eternal, something which cannot be destroyed. It has no beginning and it has no end. Dharma is the law and the code of conduct that teaches an individual how to live their life.

Hinduism encompasses a range of beliefs and customs. For a particular individual, Hinduism may mean one thing, and for another individual Hinduism may mean something slightly different; however, these two individuals are still Hindus. This aspect of freedom of thought and custom is extraordinary and makes Hinduism unique and special. However, this being said, there are common principles all Hindus generally should abide by. Many describe Hinduism as a way of life; that is because Hinduism never forces one to do anything to abide by its principles. The decisions an individual makes are personal ones, and their decisions—whether they are right or wrong—will determine their future. Consequently, when an individual states Hinduism is not a religion but a way of life, they are correct to a certain degree. This being said, there are still principles in Hinduism.

In fact, many academics argue Hinduism is the world's oldest modern day religion with scriptures such as the Rig Veda dating back to 1500 BCE (Before Common Era, i.e. Before Christ).

What is a human?

Humans are made from the five elements of earth, fire, water, air and space. Fire heats the body, water flows as blood, and the areas that are void are filled with space. As a result, when an individual passes away, the five elements that are in them return into the universe. For example, earth, fire, water, air and space within the deceased human will return to the atmosphere outside.

Demons and saints are both made from the same five elements. But if all humans are made of these elements, then why are humans different?

Humans are different due to 3 gunas (traits): Tamas, Rajas, and Sattva. Tamas means darkness. An individual living a 'Tamas' orientated life does not think about good or bad. In a similar way to how animals live, the individual merely carries out their bodily cravings. A person who lives a Tamas life not only harms themselves but also others around them.

Sattva means light of knowledge. By adopting a Sattva approach to life, a person will think about truth and justice before acting upon any decision.

Between Tamas and Sattva there is a person who possesses knowledge but does not act upon it. Such a person lives an arrogant life or, in other words, a Rajas life. The balance of these 3 gunas determines a man's nature.

When a human baby comes to life, it means the soul has entered the body. This confirms that the soul and the body are two separate entities. Most humans have the ability to function by walking, talking, and using their higher power of understanding as opposed to other life forms. However, if this is the case, we question why a human baby does not cry as soon as it leaves its mother's womb and enters the world. Why do some human babies take much longer to cry than others?

The answer to both of these questions is that a baby will not cry until the soul has entered their body; the baby is not alive until this action takes place. A soul does not always enter the baby's body immediately; hence it takes longer for some babies to start crying once born.

One may question if that is the case, then how would a foetus inside its mother's uterus be able to kick? This is a common sensation for those who are pregnant. In response to this question, the umbilical cord provides the foetus with energy from the mother to develop and grow, and this in turn leads to small movements. The question then arises, if the foetus is developing and growing which allows for small movements, does that mean a soul is within the foetus? The answer is no. After an individual passes away, sometimes the body jerks or moves suddenly. This certainly does not mean the individual is still alive or their soul is still in the body; rather this is a result of the molecules in the body slowly breaking down. In the same respect, when the foetus is growing, there will be small movements.

What is a soul?

A soul is energy within our bodies that causes the body to function. The soul is everywhere in our body, but the energy is the strongest around the heart and brain. This is the reason why these organs are vital in our functioning. For example, when we cut our nails at the tip it does not hurt us, but if we cut our nails too deep that would cause us pain. This is because the closer we get to the inside of our finger, the closer we are to our soul. In the same respect, when we pull a strand of our hair from the tip it does not pain us; however, if we pull a strand of hair from its root it does pain us. The reason for the pain is the same as in the example above.

It is not just human beings that have souls but all living organisms. A soul uses a body to operate and travel. Throughout the lifespan of a human body, the soul experiences joys and sorrows; however, it is important to understand that these emotions are not the body's—they are the soul's. A body can be destroyed but a soul cannot. There is no weapon that can pierce a soul nor can it be destroyed by any fire. The wind cannot render the soul weak nor can the wind dry the soul up.

A soul is omnipresent, intangible, and stable. In the same way that humans throw away old garments in exchange for new ones, the soul leaves a body when it has become worn out and obtains/enters a new body time and time again.

The soul is prapti (eternal); therefore, it is important to get to know your soul and understand what your soul truly is. Materialistic objects such as money, cars, wealth, clothes and even family relationships are pratiti (changing), for example, money and wealth come and go in an individual's lifetime and the choice of car we want is also constantly changing. This is not to say all of these things are not important, in particular family relationships. However, as a priority one should concentrate on understanding their soul as this is prapti (eternal).

Irrespective of the disabilities a person may have, they are still living. One who loses energy or is unconscious lives as well. For example, when an individual is in a coma their body is said to be 'dead' as it does not function. However, when they awaken after a certain period of time, they say they could hear everything but just could not talk. This illustrates how the body and the state of unconsciousness are not connected.

One who explores oneself and understands that they are not their indriyas (senses of the body), nor their body, nor feelings, nor thoughts, finally understands that he or she is in the form of a soul. This is the first step of self-realisation.

What is the purpose of a soul?

'What is the purpose of life?' This is a question often asked by mankind. However, instead of questioning the purpose of life, we should be asking: What is the purpose of the soul?

When creation took place, a fragment of God was instilled in every living being. However, our soul was clouded by desire—desire to be something in life, desire to have power, desire to have a big house, desire to have a fancy car and so forth. Awakening our soul from this desire and understanding the difference and purpose of the soul is one of life's ultimate goals. Too often people do not realise this and they live a life full of desire which entails misery. Certain humans assume feelings of life, including joy and sorrow, to be their feelings, but they are not. As stated previously, they are the body's feelings.

Human beings who do not try to discover their true self are constantly living their life in a way that will result in karma, whereby they are reborn time and time again to help awaken them.

One who understands spirituality and religion will generally have strong morals that mirror living a good and righteous life.

What righteousness is will be explained in chapter 2. This knowledge is called Brahma Vidya.

What is a sat guru?

There are many forms of gurus (teachers). Gurus are people who teach you knowledge. One of your first and most important gurus are your parents. They teach you how to walk and talk, knowledge of religion, traditions, how to be righteous, how to live a good life and so on. Another guru can be your teachers through academic education who teach you the many subjects such as maths, English and science. They impart knowledge onto you, and as a result they are teaching you something; hence you call them a guru. You can also have spiritual gurus who guides you during your lifetime. They teach you right from wrong and they answer any questions you have about religion to the best of their abilities. That is why during Guru Purnima (a religious day where people pay their respects to their gurus to show gratitude for the knowledge they have imparted) students pay respect to their gurus, their parents, their school teachers and their spiritual gurus.

As a shishya (pupil) you are thankful to a guru for sharing their knowledge. As a means of showing your thanks, a guru is highly respected and treated with much love throughout your lifetime, not only on Guru Purnima. Guru Purnima is one day where special thanks and celebrations take place.

You can have several gurus who have taught you/are teaching you; however, a sat guru is the guru who enlightens you to the ultimate truth. For example, you can have several religious gurus who have aided you in your life in uncertain situations; however, the one who reveals the ultimate truth, the one who helps you realise what you truly are, the one who enlightens you and connects you to God is called a sat guru.

Obtaining a sat guru is an essential part of life. As unacknowledged souls we need guidance and assistance on how to live life and how to control our minds. Without the proper guidance and assistance, it is very easy to walk along the wrong path of life, which will have major adverse effects on us. We would not be able to control our minds, leading us to commit sins such as lustful desires, having ill thoughts about others, jealousy or anger towards others and so on. We would form an attachment to materialistic objects like money, clothes, the television, cars, and houses, and we would have no focus in obtaining our true goal in life. We would never really achieve anything in life that holds true value. For example, as humans we are taught to be educated, do well in school, and have a good job so that we can have a comfortable life. However, money has a certain value to it, but it can only take you so far. Money cannot buy happiness, and therefore maximising the amount of money we hold is not the true aim of life. With the guidance of a sat guru, we can channel our time and efforts to reach our ultimate goal of becoming realised souls and attaining moksh (liberation from the cycle of birth and rebirth), which is explained in chapter 4.

A sat guru can show you the true path which you may have never found on your own, and for this a shishya is eternally grateful to their sat guru. As a shishya you give something of value to your sat guru. Money is just paper that has been printed on; however, this paper is valued highly in today's world and allows for the processing of all transactions around the world. Generally, the most valuable item people have is some form of wealth (money); therefore, an affordable donation is given to the sat guru by the individual in return.

Chapter 2- Dharma

What is Dharma (Righteousness)?

Essentially dharma gives an individual knowledge and purpose. It ultimately guides you on how to live life. As mentioned earlier, the first step to fulfilling dharma is understanding that you are a soul, a mere vessel, and that the body and the soul are two different entities. One who understands this is ready to start their journey towards self-realisation and fulfilling their dharma. The individual has an epiphany that creation is God and God is creation, and that there is no difference between the two.

Let us think about this statement 'creation is God and God is creation'. What does this truly mean? It means God is the creator of all beings, and in this creation lies a fragment of God, the soul. Thus, the creation is also God.

One who understands this knowledge is not cruel to other living beings, be it humans or animals. This is a key part of dharma. The individual understands amputating a limb not only causes pain to that limb but the whole body.

Similarly, when one human being feels pain, other human beings in the world also feel pain. For example, when you hear of a story of a murdered individual, a raped child, a robbery or any sort of event that has caused great pain to the people involved, do you not have sympathy for them? This feeling is compassion, which is dharma. It is a feeling we get in our gut or near our heart, and individuals who have this feeling are filled with compassion.

However, some human beings tend to forget or ignore the pain of other creatures and creations of God. This is unjust; in all creation lies a fragment of God and therefore all creations should be treated equally.

Harming people can come in many forms: lying, stealing, cheating, and abuse of various kinds such as verbal abuse, physical abuse and mental abuse. In the same way, harming other living creatures comes in many forms of violent abuse and killing.

One who is under Tamas (darkness) becomes inconsiderate, selfish and cruel to others. For their own pleasure they create sorrow upon others. They are unable to become close to God. In other words, injustice takes you away from God. They become an unrighteous individual.

God wishes to protect us and warns us not to commit sinful acts. When we are committing a sinful act, we get a feeling of fear inside of us, and it is this fear that is the message from God stating we are doing something wrong. For example, if a thief is attempting to break into a bank, they get a feeling of fear: "What if something happens?"

"What if I get caught?" In a similar way, this feeling of fear is the signal from God telling the thief that he or she is doing something wrong.

However, some individuals ignore these messages and commit the sinful act regardless. They get into a habit of ignoring this warning from God and committing sinful actions/acts. This is where punishment comes into play.

Punishment is a lesson for those who do not want to understand dharma. This way, culprits who keep committing unrighteous acts will be forced into a routine of not committing unrighteous acts. Therefore, God not only shows compassion by warning us when we act in the wrong manner but also shows compassion through punishment. For example, if a thief is caught when attempting to steal something, their punishment of being in jail will allow them to reform and think twice about committing the sinful act of stealing. We must be grateful for this act of compassion, as when injustice, ignorance and desire grow, it creates unbalance in the world and has catastrophic results. This destroys compassion and truth amongst mankind. In order for justice to prevail, punishing unjust acts is essential and inevitable.

When we carry out dharma we must ensure that we are not getting attached to the outcomes of our actions; this is called Nishkam Bhakti. To understand this you need to know the difference between deeds and actions. All deeds are actions, but all actions are not deeds. A deed is an action where an outcome is expected. When a deed is carried out expecting pleasure, wealth and praise, an individual is bound to the outcome of that action. When a deed is performed without the expectation of an outcome, it is called Nishkam Karma Yoga. In reality one is not bound by the deed—it is the expectation from a deed that binds them. This is the reason why one has to be born time and time again. Ultimately an individual should do their duty without expecting something in return, and this in effect will not bind them against that outcome.

Before Kal Yug (age of time, full explanation provided in chapter 5) started, Maha Guru Vedvyas (Great Guru Vedvyas) had written the four Vedic scriptures to ensure humans had the key principles to abide by to allow them to prosper and live a joyous life. These four Vedic scriptures are the Rig Veda, Sama Veda, Yajur Veda and Atharva Veda. However, over time the original literature set has expanded in terms of additional verses. Acharya Sri Gnane Svar Ji Arry is a regular attendee who gives religious talks on a variety of topics, such as well-being, ayurvedic medicine, diet, karma, Hindu scriptures, issues one would face in their household, etc., on the Aastha television channel. He had stated that there were 10,000 verses in the original Vedas. If you now look into the Vedas, there are more than 100,000 verses. This is significantly more than the original. The question arises as to why there are many additional verses. The answer to this is: verses have been created as manifestations.

Most of the manifestations would have been created by the Maha sages and rishimunis (great sages). This would've occurred just before Kal Yug to enable mankind to understand their dharma better during the difficult age. As time has passed, people have added subjects they think are important and issues they think need to be addressed. These subjects and issues may not be directly related to the original content of the Vedic scriptures. However, this does not make them incorrect; it simply means we need to be careful of what we read. Just how the Vedic scriptures were written to guide us on how to live a blissful life, the additional content has also been manifested to assist us in some shape or form.

It is difficult for us to know what really did happen before. We hear many stories of gods and demigods, and some of these stories may have slight differences. In the same respect we should know these stories, understand them and respect them. However, we should also understand some of them can be manifestations. There are stories that do not make sense and may make you think, *Did this really happen?* The answer is we really do not know. However, even if the stories have been manifested, they have been created to teach us something important, something vital, something that will assist us in our lives. The teaching is what we should focus on.

This is a point that is difficult for most people following Hinduism to accept and digest, and it can be easily mistranslated. Therefore, you have to be extremely careful when translating this message to someone. An individual who has a certain level of understanding about spirituality will understand this concept much quicker; one who is not familiar with spirituality and is still learning Hindu concepts/spirituality concepts can be easily misguided.

It does not mean to say Hinduism is a made up religion; it has great lessons to be learnt from these manifested stories that rishimunis would have written many thousands of years ago. You have to discover these lessons through the stories, understand them, and translate them as to what the moral of the stories are and how you can use the lessons learnt from the stories to improve your life and the lives of other living beings.

Thus far we have emphasised the importance of learning from historic events and stories such as the epic tales of the Ramayan and Mahabharat. However, one must understand it is more important to focus on ourselves as individuals to see how we can improve and understand how to awaken the God that is within us. We must not be obsessive over the stories in Hinduism. Introspect is the key to progress in your spiritual journey.

Throughout this book we will refer to such stories and the Vedic scriptures as a reference point.

There is a full explanation of the Mahabharat later in chapter 2. This is a small example in a simple context that can help us understand how manifestations are created for our understanding. In the old Mahabharat TV serials, it had shown Draupadi with one child from Arjun, named Abhimanyu. In the new Mahabharat TV serials in 2014, Draupadi was shown with five children, one from each of the Panch Pandavs. Draupadi may not have really had five sons, but in this instance this manifestation was created to illustrate an important lesson to us. This manifestation taught us what sacrifice for the greater good of the world is and how important compassion is for all other living beings. Draupadi knew her five sons would die during the Great War, Mahabharat, but their part was essential in the fight against evil. They helped attain victory but also faced death during this Maha Yud (Great War). Draupadi knew her children would die in this Maha Yud but was able to sacrifice them in order to establish righteousness. This makes us think, *What can I do to better the world? What sacrifices can I make to help and make a difference in the world?* It also helps us to understand that when aspects go wrong in our lives, sacrifices may be required in order to regain stability.

Why do you have to be careful with dharma?

Understanding dharma can be quite difficult. Knowing what to do, when to do it and what to do under unusual or demanding situations can be extremely difficult. Even individuals who are in control of their mind and have conquered their senses can make mistakes by acting in the incorrect manner, ultimately failing to fulfil their dharma.

The example we shall look at is from the Mahabharat. The Mahabharat is an epic tale of a battle between righteousness and unrighteousness, in simpler terms between good and evil. This example will detail how difficult it can be to act in the correct manner when in tricky situations. The Mahabharat is one of the most commonly used tales to show dharma and righteousness. A brief explanation of the situation is as follows. Maharaj Dhitrasth (King Dhitrasth) of Hastinapur, India was born blind but was extremely talented in warfare. He had 101 children, 100 sons and 1 daughter. Maharani Gandhari (Queen Gandhari) had been blessed by Lord Shiva (god of destruction) to have 100 sons. Her 100 sons unfortunately were evil and demonic. They held no righteous virtues and never acted according to their dharma. Duryodhan was the eldest son followed by Dushasan, who obeyed his every order. They were attempting to murder the Panch Pandavs (5 Pandavs). These were the children of Maharaj

Dhitrasth's older brother, the late Maharaj Pandu. The 100 sons had called themselves Kauravs in order to differentiate themselves from the Panch Pandavs. They did not want to be associated with the Panch Pandavs in any way, shape, or form despite being their first cousins. The Panch Pandavs were heirs to the throne and had been cheated since birth by Maharaj Dhitrasth and his sons of this right. On various occasions the 100 Kauravs had even attempted to kill the Panch Pandavs, and on one occasion even their mother, Maharani Kunti (Queen Kunti).

For reference of the example below, the characters Guru Dronacharya, Bhishma Pita, Satyavati, Yudishtr, Maharaj Shakuni and Draupadi will be explained in order to fully understand the context of the example.

Guru Dronacharya (Sage Dronacharya) was known as a Maha Guru (great guru). He was fathered by the great sage Bharadwaj muni in a clay pot. His birth was no ordinary birth which made him unique and spectacular. Guru Dronacharya was one of the most respected gurus in the whole of India. He was knowledgeable and talented in the ways of martial arts and warfare. He was the guru of the 100 Kauravs and Panch Pandavs.

Bhishma Pita (also known as Devavrata) was the son of Maharaj Shantu, the original King of Hastinapur, and goddess Ganga. Bhishma Pita was born a celestial being as he was the son of a goddess. Goddess Ganga departed from Maharaj Shantu after the birth of Bhishma Pita. She took Bhishma Pita with her to raise him to adulthood, and when he was of age he would return to his father, Maharaj Shantu. Maharaj Shantu married again to a woman belonging to a fisherman clan named Satyavati. Satyavati had certain conditions to her marriage as she was concerned for her welfare. Maharaj Shantu already had a child, Bhishma Pita; if Satyavati had conceived children with Maharaj Shantu, they would be differentiated from Bhishma Pita. In addition, they would never get a chance to be king as if Bhishma married he would rein and his children would be heirs to the throne.

During the time Maharaj Shantu wished to marry Satyavati, Goddess Ganga had returned Bhishma Pita to Maharaj Shantu. He was now of adult age, matured and grown. Bhishma Pita, upon seeing the difficult situation his father was in, promised never to marry so that his father could marry Satyavati. Upon seeing this great sacrifice, his father blessed him with the boon that he would only die when he wished to die, thus making him immortal. Also a vital piece of information to know is Bhishma Pita was the grandfather of Maharaj Dhitrasth and the late Maharaj Pandu.

Bhishma Pita had a guru who had taught him everything he knew, Bhagwan Parshuram, an avatar of Vishnu Bhagwan (god who is the preserver of life). As a result,

Bhishma Pita was extremely knowledgeable in the Vedic scriptures, righteousness and dharma, warfare and martial arts. His strength and competency was unparalleled and only a God would be able to defeat him.

Yudishtr was the oldest of the Panch Pandavs. He was renowned for his knowledge of the Vedic scriptures. He was the epitome of righteousness, truth and dharma. He never lied once in his life and always worked for the greater good. Even though the Kauravs had attempted to murder him and his family several times, he would forgive them and ask them all to live in harmony.

Maharaj Shakuni was the brother of Maharani Gandhari, Maharaj Dhitrasth's wife. Maharaj Shakuni was an evil man who had plotted to ruin Hastinapur as his sister married a blind man (Maharaj Dhitrasth) and blindfolded her eyes to be equal with her husband. Maharaj Shakuni had poisoned the minds of Maharaj Dhitrasth and his 100 sons to hate and envy the Pandavs. He had planned and plotted every attack on the Panch Pandavs and was a core culprit to the Mahabharat arising. Maharaj Shakuni had created dice out of his late father's bones and his dice obeyed every word of his. He had never lost a dice game since. This fact is pivotal in the example below.

Draupadi was the wife of the Panch Pandavs. She was born out of fire from a holy ritual. Thus she was pious and divine.

The example from the Mahabharat is as follows: Maharaj Dhitrasth and his 100 Kauravs sons came up with a cunning plan to disrespect the Panch Pandavs and disrobe their wife, Draupadi. They had invited the Panch Pandavs to Hastinapur to congratulate Yudishtr on becoming the Emperor of the Arya Region. This meant he was above in hierarchy of all the kings in the whole of the Arya Region. Hastinapur also fell into the Arya Region, meaning he was of more importance than his uncle, Maharaj Dhitrasth.

Hastinapur had organised a game of dice where betting would take place. Yudishtr had never taken part in gambling, but he did not wish to disrespect his uncle, Maharaj Dhitrasth, and so he decided to play. His opponent was Duryodhan, but his dice roller was his uncle, Maharaj Shakuni. During the game of dice, Maharaj Shakuni, as cunning as he was, asked Bhishma Pita to create the rules of the game of dice. Bhishma Pita said only money, land and property can be bet upon. Also you must have a right on what you bet and must be proud of the item you bet. The opposition must bet something of equal worth to your bet. In addition, no women were allowed to be present in the room during the game of dice as women suffer the most unrighteousness. Yudishtr and Duryodhan had both promised to abide by these rules.

Duryodhan, Maharaj Shakuni and Maharaj Dhitrasth had turned this into an attack on the Panch Pandavs. They all were aware of how the roll of the dice was always in the favour of Maharaj Shakuni. Duryodhan had initiated the betting using gold and property; however, he quickly changed this into something unexpected by all members within the room. He had started betting his brothers as part of the game. He had a right on them as he was the oldest, thus making them his property, and he was proud of them. This was greatly bending the rules set by Bhishma Pita to keep the game fair. This was an extremely low maneuver and unrighteous act betting human beings, and to make matters worse, betting his own brothers. Duryodhan and Maharaj Shakuni had cheated everyone; however, this bending of the rules meant that they were not breaking the rules either.

Yudishtr had promised to abide by the rules; therefore, he felt he could not break this promise and also decided to bet his brothers. Duryodhan had stated, "You have a right on your brothers as you are the oldest and you are proud of them; therefore, you can and must also bet them against my brothers." Duryodhan bet his wife as part of the game, and so Yudishtr also had to bet his wife. He thought he had a right on her and was proud of her, thus making it a legitimate bet as part of this game. In the end Duryodhan bet himself and in return Yudishtr had to bet himself against Duryodhan. The charm of Maharaj Shakuni on his dice had resulted in Yudishtr losing himself, his four brothers and their wife as servants to Duryodhan in the game of dice.

Duryodhan, Maharaj Shakuni and Maharaj Dhitrasth had turned this welcome banquette into an unrighteous act of betting people. Remember, the rules had been by set by Bhishma Pita, a pious and righteous man. However, his fair rules to maintain righteousness had been warped into unrighteousness.

The outcome of this game was tragic and resulted in the disrobing of Draupadi. Despite an act of unrighteousness in front of men of great valour such as Bhishma Pita, Guru Dronacharya and the Panch Pandavs, they could not defend Draupadi due to their vows and promises to let the game of dice commence. The blindness of them keeping their word had allowed an atrocity to take place. They, along with all others in the courtroom, were blinded by traditions and committed a great sin. They had all failed to truly understand dharma.

Bhishma Pita had fought his whole life against unrighteousness, Guru Drona was one of the greatest gurus in the whole of the Arya region, and Yudishtr and his brothers had fought unrighteousness all of their lives. Yet, when it counted, all of these individuals could not act to protect Draupadi. These individuals were godlike and spiritually enlightened, but were still unable to stop

Duryodhan. This proves how difficult it is to act according to dharma.

When Dushasan had walked up to Draupadi to disrobe her, she said that no one in this room can save her due to the blindness of traditions and their failure to truly act accordingly to dharma. She had prayed to the Almighty for help. Krishna Bhagwan (reincarnation of Vishnu Bhagwan) was in Dwarka at the time in a battle with soldiers attempting to overrun his kingdom; however, from there he was able to protect her. He had wrapped a piece of cloth around his finger to protect Draupadi. The event that followed in the royal courtroom of Hastinapur was a miracle and had amazed everyone. Dushasan was pulling the saree (cloth) she wore; however, regardless of how much he pulled, it seemed as if she was still wearing the saree. Dushasan was pulling and pulling and the cloth of the saree was piling up, but Draupadi still looked fully clothed. He eventually became tired and gave up. Everyone present in the courtroom knew this was a miracle of Krishna Bhagwan as no one else was capable of such a miracle.

As a result of the sin committed by all the individuals in the courtroom, those who did not protest when Draupadi was about to be disrobed were disrobed by Krishna Bhagwan. All were in shock and awe at what had happened. For Bhishma Pita, Guru Dronacharya and the

Panch Pandavs, fulfilling their oaths and promises seemed more righteous to them, but if one of them had broken their vow, then this humiliation would not have taken place.

In the Mahabharat righteousness was surrounded by malice, and righteousness surrendered before it. In other words, the understanding and context of righteousness were warped into making an unrighteous action seem virtuous. Humans make promises and oaths to better their future. For example, an individual may take the oath not to get involved in physical violence. This will allow them to stop obtaining the sin of going against ahimsa and inflicting pain upon another intentionally for no reason. This is good as it may enable the individual to become further spiritually enlightened. However, when an individual holds on to his or her oaths and promises stubbornly, it can benefit them, but is being so stubborn in every situation wise?

No, it is not. In the royal courtroom of Hastinapur when Draupadi was being disrobed, Bhishma Pita, Guru Dronacharya and even Yudishtr were bound by their oaths made to Maharaj Dhitrasth. Bhishma Pita had vowed to be the servant of Hastinapur, but only if Maharaj Dhitrasth gave the Pandavs some land to live on and make a living from as they had lost everything in this game of dice. Maharaj Dhitrasth wanted to have Bhishma Pita on his side as he would be a great asset. Bhishma Pita made a self-sacrifice of becoming a servant of Hastinapur to allow the Panch Pandavs to live a peaceful life.

Guru Dronacharya had vowed to serve Hastinapur due to an incident prior to the disrobing of Draupadi where he was leaving the royal court room of Hastinapur due to the atrocities taking place within it. His son, Ashwathama, and Duryodhan were friends since their youth, and as a result Ashwathama stayed to serve Duryodhan and assist in the atrocities taking place. Blinded by attachment to his son, Guru Dronacharya wished to stay to ensure that his son was not harmed, despite knowing this decision was wrong. The only way in which he could remain in the courtroom to look after his son was to vow to serve Hastinapur; therefore, he also became a servant of Hastinapur.

Yudishtr had vowed to abide by the rules of the game of dice, and thus the Panch Pandavs and Draupadi were the servants of Duryodhan as a result of his defeat. When he lost, he deemed it unrighteous to battle Duryodhan, as this would be going against the oath he had made. Yudishtr was the epitome of righteousness; however, he gravely misunderstood this situation and the correct action to take. He could have decided not to bet his brothers and his wife regardless of the oath he had made. He was the Emperor of the Arya Region and could do as he wished.

However, he believed fulfilling his oath was more important.

One must understand righteousness is like a tree. Oaths and promises are branches of the tree and the roots are compassion. The branches are important, but not as important as the roots. If a promise has to be broken to end one's suffering, so be it. Compassion in this situation was destroyed as they each valued their own oaths more than their love for others.

If the branches of a tree are broken off, then the branch dries up and becomes lifeless. In the same respect, there comes a time when righteousness dries up due to the lack of compassion and it becomes lifeless.

A point we must consider is that Mahabharat is one of the world's most known tales of righteousness. However, there was a point in time where it was not as widely known. People who had witnessed the Mahabharat had gone around and told stories of this epic war. Mahabharat means 'Great War'.

Throughout the ages there have been many wars; Mahabharat is one of the biggest and most exemplary ones.

There is also a 'Mahabharat' every day within each one of us. There are decisions we face daily in life that will have positive or negative consequences. For example, should one copy poor behavioral traits of their friends to be accepted into their friend circle or should the individual leave such friends and attempt to find new friends? Our good conscious is constantly battling the bad, but we must decide a course of action that is beneficial for us in the long term.

Chapter 3- Ahimsa

What is ahimsa and how does this fit into Hinduism?

Ahimsa is one of the core principles of Hinduism. It is the law of non-violence. We should coexist with all of God's creations, and only if we do this can we develop as human beings and on a spiritual level. However, if ahimsa is a core principle of Hinduism, then how can the great tales such as the Ramayan and the Mahabharat be some of the foundations of righteousness? These tales revolved around great wars, which clearly go against the principle of ahimsa.

We have already discussed what happened in the Mahabharat in chapter 2; I will now focus on the other legendary tale, The Ramayan. The Ramayan is one of the most commonly used stories in Hinduism to illustrate what dharma and righteousness are.

Maharaj Dasrath was the ruler of the land of Ayodhya. He had 3 wives, Kaushalya, Sumitra and Kei Kei. Kei Kei was Maharaj Dasrath's last wife. She had once saved Maharaj Dasrath's life when he fell ill during a battle and had treated his illness—at this time they were unmarried. In return he promised to give her 3 wishes, and regardless of what they were he would fulfil them. Her first wish was to marry Maharaj Dasrath.

Maharaj Dasrath and his wives lived happily with their four sons. Kaushalya was the mother of Ram Bhagwan, the eldest son. Sumitra was the mother of twins named Lakshman and Shatrugan. Kei Kei was the mother of Bharat, the youngest son. Over time Kei Kei's handmaiden (servant) poisoned her mind with false ideas that Maharaj Dasrath wished to overthrow her. Her handmaiden reminded her that she had two wishes still remaining to use from Maharaj Dasrath. With Kei Kei's mind poisoned and full of ill thoughts and lies, she used her second wish to banish Ram Bhagwan to the Panchavati Forest for 14 years and only after 14 years he may return. Her third wish was to crown her son, Bharat, the king. All were extremely fond of Ram Bhagwan and were saddened by this news. Ram Bhagwan was King Dasrath's favourite son, and he pleaded with Kei Kei to not do this.

Maharaj Dasrath had to send Ram Bhagwan away to the Panchvati Forest. Ram Bhagwan did not argue with his father; he simply accepted this. His wife, Sitaji, had told Ram Bhagwan she would also go with him despite the harsh living conditions of the forest. She would not be able to forsake him for 14 years. Lakshman had never been anywhere without Ram Bhagwan and had always accompanied him. He also naturally urged Ram Bhagwan to allow him to join him in his exile. In addition, with his presence he could also provide extra protection for Sitaji; therefore, Ram Bhagwan agreed.

Ram Bhagwan, Sitaji and Lakshman went to the forest for 14 years of exile. They lived in peace and harmony and their exile was very nearly over. One day a demoness called Surpanakha was in the Panchvati Forest. She was mesmorised by Ram Bhagwan and had wanted him to be her husband. Ram Bhagwan had informed her how he had already taken a vow to marry one woman in his life and he had married Sitaji. Upon hearing this, Surpanakha, full of jealousy and hatred, attempted to kill Sitaji. In order to protect Sitaji, Lakshman had strung his bow. His arrow hit Surpanakha's nose, which disintegrated from her body. Hurt and injured, she ran away to her home in Lanka (now known as Sri Lanka).

Her brother Ravan was the king of demons and ruler of the 3 worlds (Heaven, Earth and Hell). He was extremely powerful as he used to be a Shankar Bhagwan (god of destruction) bhakt (a follower of the god of destruction), and he obtained unique powers through his immense meditation. He was Shankar Bhagwan's greatest devotee, but he became so obsessed with Shankar Bhagwan that he attempted to lift Mount Kailash (where Shankar Bhagwan lived) and move it closer to Lanka. Shankar Bhagwan had warned him not to do so, but he did not heed his warning. Ravan lifted Mount Kailash, but Shankar Bhagwan forced it down by placing his foot on the mountain. Ravan's hands were stuck underneath the mountain, and Shankar Bhagwan was not letting him take them out. Ravan sang a song about the beauty of Shankar Bhagwan in order to pacify him. Shankar Bhagwan had told him he never truly understood all he had taught him, for God is everywhere. Ravan was deeply saddened as a result of the words spoken by Shankar Bhagwan, and from that day forth he never worshipped him. Despite his strength and mind power to meditate, he never truly understood righteousness. He had told everyone he now will become a god and everyone will worship him.

In his rule he had mercilessly killed many people, was a harsh and ruthless leader to his subjects, and enslaved humankind. Ravan even reined havoc amongst demigods. All were afraid to confront him. At the beginning of his reign, Shankar Bhagwan had warned him if he did not change his ways, a human being would be born to kill him. Ravan mocked Shankar Bhagwan stating, "Demigods and the Supreme Gods cannot stop me, how can a mere human stop me?"

Surpanakha returned to Lanka and informed Ravan of the events that took place in the Panchavati Forest. Ravan was enraged and wanted revenge on the people who had caused pain to his dear sister.

Ravan and his mama, Maricha, had gone to the Panchavati Forest. Maricha had forged an illusion of a beautiful golden deer outside of the hut where Ram Bhagwan, Lakshman and Sitaji lived. Sitaji had told Ram Bhagwan she had wanted this deer. The deer ran off and Ram Bhagwan ran after it. Soon after Ravan imitated Ram Bhagwan's voice shouting for help. Lakshman knew that could not be his brother for nothing could harm him; however, Sitaji got restless and urged Lakshman to go and see if his brother was ok. Lakshman was wary and did not want to leave Sitaji unprotected, so he drew a magical circle around their hut which would give Sitaji protection against any form of evil. He informed her that as long as she stayed in this circle nothing could harm her, but if she stepped out of the circle its protection would break.

Soon after Lakshman had ran off to see why he had heard Ram Bhagwan's voice shouting for help. Ravan had transformed himself into an old sage (religious person who devotes their life to God). He went to the hut asking for water. Sitaji was reluctant and the old sage reassured her that he was a man of God, and therefore it would be a sin not to give him water. Sitaji went inside her hut to fill up some water and went back outside. She explained that she could not come out of the circle, so she would pass it to him whilst standing in the circle. However, as she passed him the water her hand left the circle and the old sage grabbed her hand and pulled her out. The old sage had transformed back into Ravan. He had admired her beauty and demanded that she go with him to Lanka and be his wife. She retaliated, fought, kicked and attempted to break free, but Ravan was simply too strong. He had picked her up and put her in his golden flying chariot and flew it towards his home, Lanka. Jatayu, the King of Vultures, was a friend of Ram Bhagwan. He had seen Sitaji screaming and shouting for help and had gone to assist her. Jatayu was fighting Ravan and blocking his way. Ravan chopped his wings off and Jatayu fell from the sky to the ground.

When Ram Bhagwan and Lakshman had returned, they were astonished. Sitaji was nowhere to be found and there was a bowl lying on the ground. Ram Bhagwan and Lakshman went searching for Sitaji in the forest. When he reached the edge of the forest, he found Jatayu lying on the ground injured. He informed Ram Bhagwan of the events that took place.

Ram Bhagwan and Lakshman proceeded in the direction Jatayu had told them Ravan had gone in. On route of this path, Ram Bhagwan had met his childhood friend, Hanuman Bhagwan. Hanuman Bhagwan was the son of King Kesari and Queen Anjani, the king and queen of another ape kingdom. He was a form of Shankar Bhagwan and was blessed with many abilities by the gods. As a result, he was immensely powerful and strong. He had a god-father Pavan Dev (god of wind), and as a result Hanuman Bhagwan was as fast as the wind.

Ram Bhagwan had informed Hanuman Bhagwan of the tragedy that took place. Hanuman Bhagwan knew Ram Bhagwan would need an army to fight against Ravan's army. He suggested they proceed toward his friend Sugreeva, the King of Kishkindaa, who ruled another region (called the land of apes).

Ram Bhagwan had proceeded onwards with Hanuman Bhagwan when they met Jatayu's brother, Sampati. When hearing of his brother's death, Sampati was deeply saddened and cursed at Ravan. Being a vulture, Sampati had sharpened senses, and whilst Ram Bhagwan and Sampati were talking, Sampati heard something creeping towards Ram Bhagwan. Fearing that it was an attack on Ram Bhagwan, Sampati attacked the intruder to find that this was Ravan's brother, Vibhishan.

Vibhishan had been banished from Ravan's council for disagreeing with his evil brother's morals. Seeing how Vibhishan had been banished for fighting against unrighteousness, Ram Bhagwan asked him to accompany him on his journey to Lanka in order to free Sitaji. Vibhishan had immediately accepted his company.

Ram Bhagwan and his company had finally come to the Land of Kishkindaa, where Hanuman Bhagwan introduced them all to his friend Sugreeva, the King of Kishkindaa.

Ram Bhagwan had told Sugreeva of how Ravan had abducted Sitaji and that he needed help finding her. Sugreeva had informed Ram Bhagwan that Ravan lived in Lanka, the island of gold. It was called the island of gold as the earth was rich in gold in Lanka.

They had proceeded to the edge of the forest and there was the Laccadive Sea in between Lanka and India. Ram Bhagwan had instructed Hanuman Bhagwan to fly over the sea in an attempt to find Sitaji. Before he left, Ram Bhagwan had given Hanuman Bhagwan his ring so that Sitaji would know Hanuman Bhagwan was on his side. He encountered many obstructions on the way such as demon sea monsters. When he reached Ravan's palace, he found Sitaji in the royal gardens. He hid in a nearby tree, and upon hearing Sitaji crying for Ram Bhagwan, he was filled with sorrow. He dropped the ring Ram Bhagwan had given him into Sitaji's lap, and she demanded to see who had her lord's ring. Hanuman Bhagwan showed himself and explained how Ram Bhagwan was looking for her. She had insisted that Ram Bhagwan was to come to Lanka in person and collect her rather than escaping with Hanuman Bhagwan. Sitaji blessed him to have a successful journey.

Soon after, he bid Sitaji farewell and she blessed him once more. She told him to give her bangles to Ram Bhagwan, knowing that he would recognise them and know she is safe. Hanuman Bhagwan flew back to Ram Bhagwan and informed him of the events that took place in Lanka.

Ram Bhagwan knew it was more crucial than ever to rescue Sitaji. He demanded the sea to part in order to let his army through. This action angered the Sea God and a storm started in the sea. Ram Bhagwan warned the Sea God to calm down or he would dry up the entire Earth's oceans with a single strike of his arrow. The sea calmed and the Sea God came before them. He apologised as he did not recognise Ram Bhagwan's true form (a reincarnation of Vishnu Bhagwan, the preserver of the worlds). The Sea God stated they were not able to divide the sea to create a path. The Sea God advised Ram Bhagwan that if he wrote the holy name of Ram Bhagwan on the rocks nearby the sea they would float. Ram Bhagwan had tried this and it worked. In this manner, placing rock after rock, an entire bridge was made from India to Lanka. This bridge is now called Ram Sethu and is famous. It still partially exists and satellite pictures from space show the bridge. This is now a popular place of pilgrimage.

Ram Bhagwan proceeded with his army across the bridge and entered Lanka. This is when the war began. Ravan's youngest son, Meghnaath, had approached Ram Bhagwan. He was a trickster and created the illusion that Sitaji had been beheaded by Ravan. Meghnaath created an illusion of Sitaji's head dripping with blood and exclaimed to Ram Bhagwan, "You had come for your wife. Take back your wife, here, take her!" Ram Bhagwan had emotionally broken down and was crying. Vibhishan had informed Ram Bhagwan this was a mere illusion, and Ram Bhagwan and his army proceeded towards the palace.

Ravan had become even more desperate to win this war and awakened his half-brother, who also happened to be a giant. His name was Kumbhakarana. Kumbhakarana had a reputation for being a brute when it came to warfare. As per Ravan's instructions, he headed to the battlefield without hesitation to fight Ram Bhagwan. As Kumbhakarana stepped onto the battlefield, Hanuman Bhagwan had noticed that he towered over all and personally offered to fight him. Hanuman Bhagwan grew thrice in size to match Kumbhakarana and defeated him after a vigorous battle.

With all of Ravan's best men defeated, he had no option but to physically step onto the battlefield and confront Ram Bhagwan. Ram Bhagwan knew that the source of Ravan's power was a potion that he had kept in his stomach. As a result, Ram Bhagwan shot an arrow at

Ravan's stomach, piercing his flesh and causing the potion to release.

Ravan had a flashback of Shankar Bhagwan foretelling how a mere human would defeat his evil reign. With this in mind, he realised Ram Bhagwan was God and asked for forgiveness whilst dying.

Ram Bhagwan had won the war; Ravan was dead and humankind was free once more. By the time the war was over, Ram Bhagwan's 14 years of exile had been completed. He was now allowed to go back to Ayodhya. A message was sent to Ayodhya informing the royal family that Ram Bhagwan would return home. The citizens of Ayodhya knew it would be nightfall by the time Ram Bhagwan, Sitaji and Lakshman would return, so they all lit divas (oil wick lamps) outside their homes to guide them. The light represents righteousness and the truth dominating over evil. This is why on Diwali it is common for those celebrating the festival to light divas (oil wick lamps) inside their homes.

Now that the story of Ramayan has been explained, I will now illustrate how the principle of ahimsa fits into these great wars. In the Ramayan and Mahabharat there were evil forces which caused havoc. In the Ramayan it was Ravan, and in the Mahabharat it was the 100 Kauravs. In both cases the righteous party had issued a message of non-violence, but the unrighteous and sinful party (Ravan and the 100 Kauravs) deliberately opposed this message. In the Ramayan, Hanuman Bhagwan travelled to Lanka to order Ravan to give Sitaji back; otherwise, there would be war. In the Mahabharat, the Pandavs gave the Kauravs numerous chances to repent their sinful acts and they chose not to. Despite these warnings, Ravan and the 100 Kauravs continued sinful and selfish acts. Selfishness, pride and ego had blinded them. They lived their lives and acted for their self-benefit.

In this situation the principle of righteousness was not being followed, and unrighteous people were committing terrible acts. Thus, the war that occurred was necessary for the welfare of the world. In such a situation, ahimsa (the law of non-violence) had already been disregarded by Ravan and the 100 Kauravs. This war would restore the balance of peace, returning humankind to its natural peaceful state. This war was necessary to establish righteousness once again; therefore, it was a dharma yud (righteous war). If the principle of ahimsa has to be broken to establish true righteousness, then so be it—the end goal of establishing righteousness is far greater.

In the Mahabharat 2014 TV serials, the actor playing Krishna Bhagwan stated, "An unrighteous act for righteousness cannot be unrighteous." Therefore, after giving several chances to Ravan and the 100 kauravs showing them the true path did not work, waging war was the only option. All other methods had been tried and were fruitless.

We must remember to not take this out of context. Righteousness is truth. This cannot be warped with human beings making up their own rules and meanings. Our conscience tells us what is wrong and what is right, what is sinful and what is righteous. We have that fearful feeling and guilty conscience when we are committing a sinful or wrong act. That is God telling us that we are doing something wrong.

A point we must consider is that even in the Ramayan and Mahabharat the leaders of both armies would have had to do some sort of penance to repent for the killings even if the aim was to establish righteousness. In order to establish righteousness and truth, sacrifice was needed. Only those brave and noble enough are able to make this sacrifice.

However, it is important to understand that it is not always necessary to wage war in order to establish righteousness. Starting from the 1750s, India was under the British rule. During this time many atrocities took place which undermined the population of India—slavery, abuse and poor living standards just being a few of them. For 197 years India was under the rule of the British. On October 2nd, 1869 in Porbandar, India, a boy was born who would later free India from this state; his name was

Mohandas Karamchand Gandhi. He is better known now as Mahatma Gandhi.

Mahatma Gandhi studied law at a university in London and worked as a lawyer in South Africa opposing discrimination against Indians. In 1914 Mahatma Gandhi moved back to India to oppose the British rule. He had a vision of a free India and fought for this vision using his skills as a lawyer. He had fought for the freedom of India between 1919-1922 and was later jailed for conspiracy from 1922-1924. In 1930, he led a march to the sea to collect salt in symbolic defiance of the government monopoly and was again jailed in 1931.

Mahatma Gandhi had motivated and inspired citizens throughout India not to physically fight against the British but to fight against them using the power of ahimsa (non-violence). Hundreds upon hundreds of citizens simply blocked roads, lying on the ground to obstruct vehicles and protest. The British started shooting at citizens, running them over with vehicles, and moving them out of the way using firehoses, but the citizens did not move. Many people had died, but in the end the British could not justify these people being killed as they were not fighting back. As a result of this movement, the British left India in 1947 and Mahatma Gandhi became the founding father of a free India.

Thus we must analyse the situation we are in and decide accordingly how we can establish righteousness. Even in the case of the independence of India, there were huge sacrifices made in order to establish righteousness. Someone has to guide the establishment of righteousness and be the beacon of light people look for, and these are the people that are remembered for their greatness.

In every situation it is best to avoid using violence. It should only be used as a last resort after many attempts for a peaceful resolution, as illustrated in the epic tale of the Mahabharat.

Why do most Hindu gods hold weapons in their pictures?

There are many stories of gods in Hinduism which we hear and use as a method of learning about Hinduism. Some of the aspects we learn about are what righteousness is, what evil is, what life is, what sacrifice is and so on. Many of these stories revolve around gods and demigods defeating evil and returning the world to a natural state of peace. For example, Ramayan and Mahabharat are two of the most profound stories which we have discussed in this book, but there are many more stories involving gods such as Shankar Bhagwan (Lord Shiva), Ganpati Bhagwan (elephant god), Brahma Bhagwan (god of creations).

In all of these stories good overcame evil; therefore, in most of the pictures of gods they are holding weapons of some sort. Some pictures also feature animals alongside a god. For example, in Ganpati Bhagwan's photo it is the norm to see mice alongside him in the picture. This signifies how all creatures are valued in the eyes of God and not only humans.

However, it is crucial to remember that these pictures are a fragment of our imagination. God does not really look like how they do in the pictures as no one has seen God's true form. A few people may have seen God in a different form, i.e. not their true form but their form as a human, whilst others may have experienced being at one with God. These pictures help us to focus on the gods and imagine their divinity and supremeness. This point will be further discussed in chapter 6.

It is good that people pray; however, not many people can focus and pray to God without visualising God, hence the purpose of murtis and photos. The next level above that is when one understands that these images are not God's true form and God is everywhere, and as a result they can pray without the need of visualising God. This is difficult to do and comes with time, focus and meditation upon God.

Why should we not eat meat?

In Hinduism eating meat is forbidden. It goes against the principles of ahimsa (non-violence). We have a choice whether to slaughter an animal for food or not. In the same respect you can either decide to eat meat or you can decide not to eat meat. But the question arises: Why would you choose to slaughter animals for food?

There is plenty of other food besides meat to eat. People who consume meat ask with concern: But what do you eat if you are vegetarian? There are several types of meats; in the same respect there is a vast amount of different types of beans, pulses, vegetables and fruits. They are all cooked in different ways in different cuisines. Therefore, the claim that one must consume meat as there is a lack of variety in other foodstuffs cannot be justified.

People who consume meat also claim it is good for you as it is high in protein. There are plenty of other options for protein for the matters of health and fitness. Substitutes include soya milk, almond milk, tofu, Quorn, a variety of beans and pulses and many meat-free substitutes made to taste similar to meat which are high in protein. Furthermore, the body does not use all the protein obtained from eating meat and the excess protein is urinated out or is excreted through sweating. Thus, those with high protein diets may notice a smell similar to ammonia in their urine. In addition, staying hydrated is a challenge for people who have a high intake of protein as an excessive amount of protein requires water to break it down.

In fact, eating meat results in higher probabilities of getting ill. A study carried out by the BBC showed Professor Walter Willett, of the Harvard School of Public Health, heading a team that was tracking the diets of tens of thousands of people for many years. In his findings it was shown that those who consumed higher amounts of red meat had a higher risk of total mortality, cardiovascular mortality and cancer mortality. Furthermore, he had found that eating processed meat, such as bacon, ham or salami, had a negative impact on health.

In addition, The Guardian had carried out a research study where high levels of dietary animal protein in people under 65 years of age were linked to a fourfold increase in their risk of death from cancer or diabetes, and almost double the risk of dying from any cause over an 18-year period. However, further research needs to be carried out to understand why this is.

Furthermore, illnesses such as viral and bacterial infections can be provoked by natural causes, for example mad cow disease. Illnesses can also arise from undercooked meat, the poor living conditions of animals and the maturing of meat.

Ultimately, the question arises again as to why a person would slaughter an animal for food. We've already established that it is not due to the lack of nutrients found in other food, and so therefore it must be due to the taste of the meat itself.

However, the killing of animals for self-indulgence is considered morally wrong. God has created all living beings including animals, therefore there is a part God within each animal called Paramatma (explained in chapter 6). Animals are equally as important as humans. With this in mind, how can it be right that an animal is killed for the consumption of food?

Animals have 5 senses, they can move, and they have a brain to think and a conscience. The only difference is they cannot talk the human language and cannot control their minds to the degree human beings can. Animals are known to sense disasters before they even occur; thus their minds may be advanced in ways we cannot comprehend. Nevertheless they still feel fear, they still feel pain and they cry.

Generally, the way in which animals are treated is extremely wrong. They are kept in small cages with many other animals where there is no room to move. These animals can catch diseases from each other. Some die due to the dire living conditions, and the ones who remain alive suffer from severe injuries only to be killed a few hours later. The animals that die after suffering from diseases are still used for food consumption.

Furthermore, they are beaten for no reason, abused, kicked and then ruthlessly killed. There are many videos online about the process of this.

The question then arises as to how you can consume meat after knowing how the animal lived its life and was killed.

Let us think of this in terms of spirituality. When an animal is being prepared for slaughter, it must be frightened, anxious and trying to fight back. It would secrete testosterone to help in this battle for life. After it has been killed, all of this negative energy stays within its body.

The last thing the animal remembers is a knife slashing their throat and feeling pain. The animal's body, which is full of pain, anger, negative thoughts and energy, is then prepped for consumption. When one eats meat they also consume the pain, anger, negative thoughts and energy. This can affect the behaviour and temperament of the individual consuming the meat.

Brahmakumaris is an organisation which started in 1937 that has knowledge about the nature of the soul, of God and of time, concepts so simple in their expression but so profound in meaning that they awakened a powerful sense of recognition in those with whom the visions were shared. They found a piece of research which had astonishing results. A Japanese scientist had carried out an experiment where he cooked food in different types of moods, for example, happy, sad, angry and so on. He found the molecular structure of all of the food cooked was different depending on the mood that he was in. This shows you how powerful your energy and thoughts are. It makes a huge difference. Therefore, imagine the negative energy you consume when you eat meat.

Albert Einstein was a Nobel Prize winner for physics in 1921. The practical applications of Einstein's theories include the development of the television, remote control devices, automatic door openers, lasers, and DVD players. Einstein stated, "Nothing will benefit health and increase the chances of survival on Earth as the evolution to a vegetarian diet." There was a time when he adopted a vegetarian's diet and stated, "So I am living without fats, without meat, without fish, but am feeling quite well this way. It always seems to me that man was not born to be a   carnivore."
If great minds like Einstein were saying such things, there must be truth in this.

To further clarify Einstein's point, we will look at the following analogy. The primary reason for all animals being eaten is to gain energy; we must bear this in mind when looking at the following analogy. There is some lettuce, a fly eats some of the lettuce, a frog eats the fly, and a hawk eats the frog. As each organism consumes their food, the energy transferred is drastically reduced (approximately 8%-10% of energy is transferred from one being to another). All other energy (90%-92%) is used by the organism for respiration, i.e. staying alive, excreting, etc. Therefore, it would make perfect sense not to consume organisms higher up the food chain as less energy is transferred. It is much more efficient to consume the producer (plantation) as this provides the greatest energy transfer. The energy consumption values are given as approximate examples:

5kJ

50k

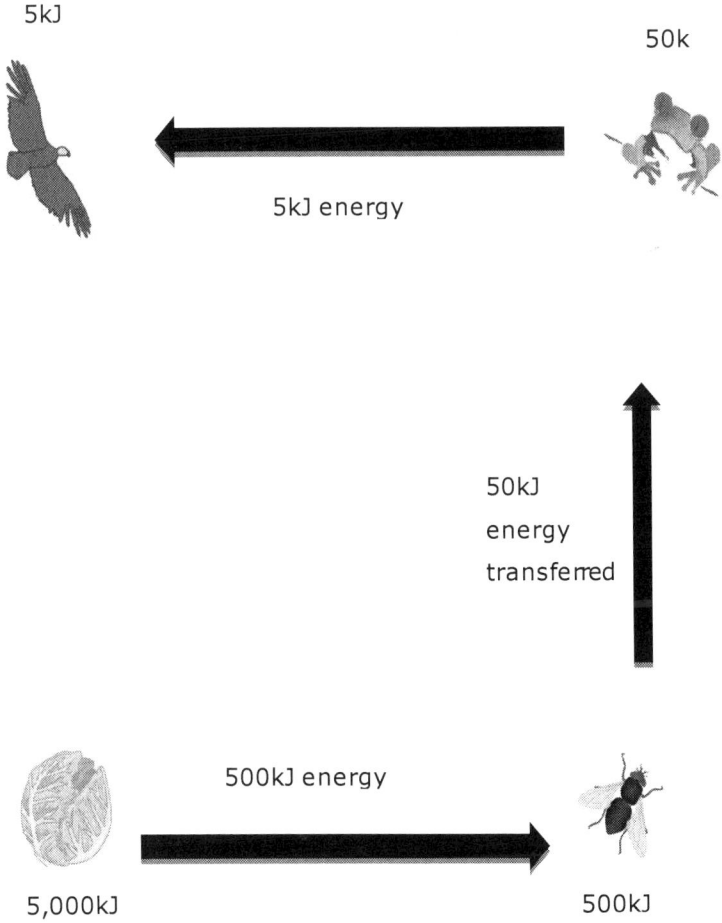

5kJ energy

50kJ
energy
transferred

500kJ energy

5,000kJ

500kJ

Chapter 4- Karma and Reincarnation

What is karma and reincarnation?

What is karma and how does it work?

Karma is a concept that is widely accepted in the world. It is a topic that is deep and intense; however, it is essential to understand its principles for then one realises how important their actions become. Understanding karma helps when dealing with problems and suffering, and it helps us decide how we want to live our lives. In the modern day there is a saying: "What goes around comes around." This was derived from the principles and meaning of karma.

Karma is derived from the Sanskrit word 'kr' meaning to act. Any act an individual carries out will have a resultant karma. For example, walking, thinking, and eating are all actions that can have resultant karmas. For every action there is a resultant fruit (outcome) which is either good or bad. The deciding factor which determines if the resultant fruit is good or bad is the nature of the action. Auspicious karmas yield good fruits and bad karmas yield bad fruits.

The fruit of karma can be received instantly or it will ripen over time and will be received either later in life or in another life.

Types of karma

There are three types of karma, which are Sanchit karmas, Prabhada karmas and Kriyaman karmas. Sanchit karmas are karmas that are stored as they do not give an instant fruit and need time to ripen. These karmas can be from both previous lives as well as the present. Prabhada karmas are karmas that have ripened and the fruit can be acknowledged. These distinguish the fate of the individual in this lifetime, for example, diseases, lifespan, happiness, sadness, etc. all are outcomes of Prabhada karmas. Kriyaman karmas are those performed every day in the present lifetime, and the fruit is received instantly or very soon after. For example, if a thief is looting a shop and is caught and arrested shortly after, this would be the fruit of his Kriyaman karma.

The reason why karma is a crucial aspect to understand is because it gives knowledge and understanding as to why we experience the occurrences that take place in our life. When things go wrong or misery is upon us, we as humans blame other individuals and God. "Oh God, why are you doing this to me?" we ask. All of the things that occur in our life are as a result of our actions that result in karma and the fruit of that outcome. We must understand that there is no one to blame but ourselves. It is similar to paying off an old debt—once the debt is paid that record is clean. Accepting this helps one deal with the calamities in life.

Head and Cranston (1970) stated that "those who believe in karma have to believe in destiny, which from birth to death, every man is weaving, thread by thread, around himself, as a spider does his cobweb...karma creates nothing, nor does it design. It is man who plants and creates causes and karmic principle adjusts the effects...he who unveils through study and meditation its intricate paths, and throws light on those dark ways...is working for the good of his fellow men..."

We shall refer to a real life example from *Karma and Reincarnation in Hinduism* (2012). It refers to a story Hiralal Thakkar wrote about in his book, *Karma Siddhant*. In the mid-twentieth century, a judge witnessed a man being murdered in Ahmedabad (the capital of the state of Gujarat, India) on the shore of the River Sabarmati. The judge did not inform anyone of this as he knew this case would end up in his court and he would prosecute the murderer when they met. The police brought the man in for the trial of the victim's murder. The judge was shocked as this was not the man at the scene of the crime. The judge was a scholar of Vedanta and knew the principle of karma never fails; therefore, he summoned the man to his room. The judge stated that he was aware that this person did not commit the murder. The man said he knew who did it. The man informed the judge of how he was innocent and how the police had created 'fake' evidence to make it seem like they caught the culprit. The judge was convinced that the principle of karma never fails and thus questioned the man, "Did you ever murder anyone in the past?" The man with tears in his eyes explained he was once rich and wealthy and had killed two people. He had paid large sums of money to the police and lawyers to cover this up. The judge explained how his past karma had created a fruit. The fruit did not ripen for him to be prosecuted then, but now this had caught up with him. Even though he was innocent for the murder in question now, he was guilty for the murder he committed many years ago.

This example proves how all of our actions have an outcome, a fruit, a consequence. Even though we may not see it immediately or in this lifetime, it definitely will come out when the fruit of your outcome has ripened.

We will not dwell on the evidence of reincarnation too much but will provide a few examples to prove its existence. The following examples are from *Karma and*

Reincarnation in Hinduism by Sadhu Mukundcharandas of BAPS Swaminarayan Sanstha.

Things that do not incur karma

Animals and insects do not receive any karma for the actions they carry out. They do not have the mind control and advanced functions that human beings have and therefore cannot differentiate between wrong and right. Humans do have this capability; therefore, our actions have resultant karmas.

Babies and very young children or mentally ill people do not incur pap karma (bad karma) as they do not have the understanding of what is wrong and right. For example, if a young child stepped on insects, they would be scolded by his or her parents, but this action would not result in pap karma. Babies and young children learn over time what is wrong and what is right as they transcend into later life. Mentally ill people may not have the understanding they require in order to differentiate between right and wrong; therefore, they also do not incur pap karma.

Rebirth as humans or animals?

The type of living creature an individual is reborn as depends on the karma of the individual. For an individual to be reborn as a human being would be as a result of great punya karma (good karma) as the human life form is the highest entity one can be reborn as. A human is classed as the highest entity as we can control our thoughts and consciousness, and use our higher intellect as we wish. No other living creature is able to do this on planet Earth.

In the same respect, it is possible for one to be reborn as any type of animal. This is classed as a lower level entity due to them not being able to use their intellect as humans can.

Some say if you are born a human then you cannot be reborn as any other living entity. However, if this is the case, then why has the human population been rapidly increasing since the creation of the earth?

It is widely believed that if an individual is reborn as an animal they have to go through rebirth as each type of animal before they can attain a human birth again. There are several million animals on this planet, and as a result that is why human life is valued so greatly.

How to avoid rebirth

The sanchit pool is where our karmas are left to ripen. Until this sanchit pool is empty of our karmas we cannot stop the cycle of birth and rebirth. When the cycle of rebirth is stopped, this is called attaining moksh. Moksh means liberty and being at one with God all the time. This should be the main aim of one's life.

All of our actions have a resultant karma that attaches itself to us. If a good action is performed, for example donating to the poor, then a good outcome will occur. Similarly, if a bad action is performed, for example stealing, a bad outcome will occur. Therefore, the question arises how one can actually attain moksh. In this case the sanchit pool seems ever growing. There are actions that do not cause outcomes, such as praying, kirtan (devotional songs), satsang (religious discussion), doing sewa (helping people) and chanting God's name.

The most important aspect to consider is performing these acts in a selfless manner so that we are not bound to the outcome. In chapter 2 we mentioned the following sentence: In reality a man isn't bound by the deed; it's the expectation from a deed which is what binds him. I.e., do your duty without expecting something as this won't bind you. Ultimately if we carry out these good actions for God and not for our own benefit, we cannot be bound to these actions. However, if we perform them for ourselves, we will bind the outcome to us; therefore, reincarnation into another life is inevitable.

Furthermore, a point one must consider is what you think of at the time of death is very important. At the time of death, as the soul leaves the body, the last thought on your mind leaves an imprint on the soul. For example, if you were thinking of your parents, there is a very good chance you can be reborn to the same parents in this life or the next. Therefore, thinking of God is essential as this ensures you have a greater chance of being one with God after death.

Reincarnation stated in the Shastras (religious texts)

Vedas

"O father! Let the divine being grant us the mind in the birth with which we can endeavor for knowledge, truth and other virtues."

Rig Veda 10/57/5

Upanishads

"The fool who is blinded by wealth and engrossed in indulgence is unable to strive for parlok (heaven). Those who believe in the existence of only this world but not heaven, attain me (Yama Raja (god of death)) repeatedly."

Katha Upanishad 1/1/6

"Just as a goldsmith beats gold to create new and beautiful forms, similarly the atma (soul) sheds this body to make a new one for moksha. This (body) belongs to pitrus, gandharvas, devas, Prajapati Brahma or other beings (God/divine beings)."

Bruhadarayanyaka Upanishad 4/4/4

"As his karmas and actions, so his next birth. By pious karma he becomes pious. By evil karmas he becomes evil."

Bruhadarayanyaka Upanishad 4/4/5

Bhagvat Gita

Vasamsi jiranani yatha vihaya, navani gruhnati naro-parani.

Tatha sharirani vihaya jirnanyani samyati navani dehi.

(2/22)

"As a person discards old clothes and adorns new ones, similarly, he discards old bodies and enters new ones."

Bahuni me vyatitani janmani tava charjuna tanyaham veda servani na tvam vettham paramtapa.

(4/5)

"O Arjuna! You and I have taken many births. I remember them all; you do not."

Yam yam vapi smaranbhavam tyajatyante kalevram, tam tamevaiti kaunteya sada tadbhavabhavitah

(8/6)

"Arjuna, thinking of whatever entity one leaves the body at the time of death, that and that alone one attains, forever absorbed in its thoughts."

Yog Vashishta Ramayana (Yog Vashishta was the guru of Ram Bhagwan)

"Just as birds fly from one tree to another, similarly jivas bound by hope and countless desires leave one body and enter another."

(4/43/26)

Past lives stated in the Shastras

Sati Parvati:

In reference to the Shiva Purana, Devi Bhagvat and Shrimad Bhagvatam (all of these are sacred texts), Sati was the daughter of Daksha and the first consort of Shiva. She immolated herself (sacrificed herself in fire) in Daksh's yagna. She was reborn to Himvan Parvat and Menka. She was named Parvati.

Dasrath and Kaushalya

The Ramacharitmanas of Tulsidas (sacred text) states that Kashyap Rishi and Aditi were reincarnated as King Dasrath and Kaushalya, the parents of Ram Bhagwan.

Jadbharat

In the Shrimad Bhagvatam (5th Skandh – sacred text) there is a very well-known story of King Bharat, the son of Bhagwan Rishabhdeva. King Bharat had forsaken his kingdom to perform taap (penance) in the forest. During his penance he became attached to a fawn (young deer). As a result, he was born to a deer in his next life and the life after that he was born as a Brahmin called Jadbharat. Jadbharat narrates his life to King Rahugan:

"O Rahugan! In my past life I was a king named Bharat. I forsook worldly desires to offer devotion to Paramatma. But I became attached to a fawn and fell from my path of sadhana (spirituality) and was born as a deer. By devotion to Shri Krishna as a deer I was able to remember my life as King Bharat. Now I keep myself aloof from people and roam around in secret."

Prahalad

The Padma Purana provides details of Prahalad narrating his past life. He was called Somsharma, son of Shivsharma of Dwarka. He was a devotee of Vishnu, offering devotion day and night in Harihar Kshetra. A gang of demons came to disturb his devotion. As he was dying he recalled the demons. Therefore, he was born to the demon Hiranyakashipu in his next life as Prahalad.

Reincarnation examples

The following case is in regards to the Pollock Twins from England. This case illustrates how two sisters died together and were born again to the same parents. On the 5th of May, 1957, Joanna aged eleven and Jacqueline aged six, born of John and Florence Pollock of Hexam, both died instantly when a car smashed into them. John, who was a Roman Catholic, believed in reincarnation and wished for them to be reborn, despite his wife not sharing his belief.

Approximately a year later Florence gave birth to twin girls whom they called Gillian and Jennifer. Upon looking at Jennifer, John noticed a thin white line on her forehead. Jacqueline had the same thin scar after she cut her head when she was two years old. Florence had noticed a brown birthmark on Jennifer's left hip, which was the same size, shape and in the same position as Jacqueline had.

Later in life John and Florence Pollock received absolute confirmation that their daughters had been reborn. After the tragedy of the accident, John and Florence had moved from Hexam to Whitley Bay. When the twins were three years old, John and Florence took them to Hexam for a day trip. As they walked around they listened to the twin's conversation in awe. "The school's just around the corner," "That's where we used to play in the playground," "The swings and slides are over there" (out of sight behind a hill). When they passed their old house, the twins exclaimed, "We used to live there!"

John and Florence had kept some old toy dolls that Joanna and Jacqueline once played with. One night they put the toys outside of the twins' room and watched in amazement as the twins seized them and handled the toy that belonged to each in their previous birth, remembering the dolls' names. "This is my Suzanne." "That's Mary. I haven't seen her for a long time!"

Once the twins were playing in a nearby street and John rushed out hearing their screams. He saw them clutching each other pointing to a car which had just started. "The car! The car! It's coming at us!" It seems the twins were frightened of the car crashing into them as it did in their previous life.

Dr Ian Stevenson worked in the department of psychiatry at the University of Virginia School of Medicine. He is renowned for his work on reincarnation and the evidence of its existence. (http://www.iisis.net/index.php?page=semkiw-ian-stevenson-reincarnation-past-lives-research). He was particularly interested in reincarnation cases with birthmarks. This provided biological evidence of a metaphysical occurrence (how the soul takes a temp body form as it passes on into the next life) and the reason why certain inheritance could not be explained by genetic inheritance. In Hinduism after one passes away there is an eleven day process where bhajans (hymns and religious songs) are held. It is believed by some that each day the temporary body grows new limbs until the 11th day where the temporary body is fully formed. If this is the case, it ties in with Dr Stevenson's theory of a metaphysical occurrence.

The following case is of an individual named Pal Jatav. Dr Stevenson had researched this case. Pal Jatav was a boy born in December 1971 in a village called Nagla Devi, in the Mainpuri District of Utarpradesh. He was born with stubbed fingers on his right hand, but his left hand was normal. When he was around the age of one and a half, he spoke of a previous life in Tal Gaon (Gaon means village). He once revealed that he (as Hukam Singh in a previous life) and his chacha (uncle) were cutting fodder in a machine. While pushing stalks in it, his right hand was crushed.

When Pal visited Tal Gaon (Nagla Tal) and met the family members of Hukam Singh, he recognised Bharat Singh as his brother and Raj Ranias his mother. He also recognised Hukam Singh's brothers and sisters and correctly pointed to where the fodder machine had been.

Later, Dr Pasricha had X-rayed Pal's hands. After analysing this, Dr Stevenson stated that although Pal suffered from the birth defect brachydactyly, no members in his family on both of his parents' sides or in the past two generations had any similar birth defects. In medical books bilateral brachydactyly (short bones resulting in short fingers and toes) has been found to be a transmitted birth defect. The unilateral (single hand or foot affected) type is even more uncommon. Dr Stevenson has only found one published case where the patient had short fingers, but this is still different to Pal's case. Pal had boneless stubs. Dr Stevenson later described an additional unilateral case in Burma, similar to Pal's, where the fingers of an individual were slashed in their previous life.

Child prodigies

There are some stories in the world whereby children at very young ages have enhanced intelligence, maturity, bhakti (devotion), and artistic and musical talents. But how can this be? How can a person at such a young age obtain such talents? Karma and reincarnation is the answer to this question. The reason why an individual can obtain such a talent at a young age is because they had knowledge of it in their previous life and maybe even in previous lives before that. There must be a reason why they have retained that knowledge into their next life, a deep root cause. We can only speculate what the root cause is as all actions of the individual will result in a type of karma. It could take vast amounts of time and research to come to the conclusion of the case.

I will now go through a list of examples of some child prodigies:

Wolfgang Mozart: music's wonder child. He portrayed his musical talents since childhood. At the age of three he played the piano. At the age of four he started learning the violin. He started writing music notation at the age of six. At the age of seven he composed a full length opera.

Christian Heinecken: born in Germany in 1721. He talked within a few hours of his birth. He spoke Latin and German by the age of three. He gave lectures on the Bible, history and geography. Amazingly, he predicted his own death at four and died in 1725, four years after his birth.

Adi Shankaracharya: a world renowned Hindu philosopher born in 788 AD. He was famous for his understanding and interpretations of Hindu religious scriptures. He studied the four Vedas by 8 years old, mastered the Shastras by 12 years old, and by 16 years old wrote commentary on Upanishads, Bhagvat Gita and Prasthantrayi- Brahma Sutras.

How can children of such young ages achieve these amazing outcomes that even fully grown adults who have studied in their respective fields struggle with? It cannot be genetic inheritance, and even the children of genius parents rarely turn out to be like their parents.

Environmental conditioning cannot be the answer as how much conditioning can occur in children at such young ages of three to four?

There is a myth that a human only uses 10% of their brainpower. But no sources can verify where this fact is sourced from. There are several questions raised such as: 10% of what overall amount? A human uses only 10% of their brain when? When sleeping, walking or eating?

It is assumed human beings of great talent, such as child prodigies, use a greater capacity of their brain. This is correct; however, the rule that a human being only uses 10% of their brain is not. An individual can only attain such unique abilities through brain control, meditation and being one with God. Therefore, the reason behind individuals having these abilities is brain control and meditation. However, this is no easy task. It takes a lifetime to gain the ability to control your mind. As a result, that is why very few individuals have such unique abilities. These individuals have these abilities due to past life endeavors, not because they were born with such a gift.

Xenoglossy and xenography

Xenoglossy and xenography are very interesting terms. Xenoglossy is when people speak a language they have never learnt before. Xenography is when people write a language they have never learnt before. Below we will cite a few examples of such cases that occurred.

Head & Cranston (1994) had found an interesting case of a New York physician, Dr Marshall McDuffie. He was the father of two twin boys. The two twin boys were conversing in an unknown and mysterious language. Dr McDuffie had taken them to Columbia University's department of foreign languages to distinguish what language they were talking. However, none of the experts he consulted could identify what dialect they were conversing in. By chance another professor of ancient languages was passing by and had identified it as Aramic, a language spoken during the first century in the Middle East.

For the purpose of the next example, the concept of past life regression theory will be explained. Past life regression theory is where psychologists use hypnosis to retrieve memories of an individual which date back to a previous birth. Fisher (1993) found a Canadian psychologist who spoke Norsk, a predecessor of the modern day Icelandic language, whilst under regression theory. This language was spoken around 1000 AD. Thereafter he described himself as a man in Mesopotamia, Persia in 625 CE. He then wrote down a script later identified as Sassanid Pahlavi. This form of writing has been extinct since 651 AD.

The next example is from the sect of Hinduism, BAPS Swaminarayan. Parth Modi was born on the 5th September, 2005. He was born in Ahmedabad, in the state of Gujarat to Gujarati parents. When Parth first began to talk, roughly at the age of 2 and a half, he spoke Hindi. None of his family members converse in Hindi and all speak Gujarati. The family was shocked and surprised. Whenever people converse with Parth, he always responds in Hindi. After analysing Parth's Hindi, experts have confirmed he speaks Hindi spoken in Lucknow (the capital city of the state Uttar Pradesh, India). They also deduced that some of his actions are rather mature. Parth has never spoken about a previous life. His grandfather had said that as Parth grew up he came up with new and amazing Hindi words and phrases.

Parth has a strong aversion to learning or conversing in Gujarati with his parents or school friends. This ties in with the findings of Dr Stevenson. He found many cases where Burmese parents had given birth to children with blue eyes and blonde hair with Mongolian features and dark skin. The children claimed to have been American pilots shot down by the Japanese over Burma during World War

II in their previous life. They resisted speaking Burmese during early childhood (Stevenson, 1997).

Dreams

Science is still unable to provide a concrete theory that explains what the purpose of dreams is and why it is human beings dream. However, science can verify dreams work in cycles of sleep, and this is linked to brain activity. But where does the brain acquire such creativity to concoct such vivid and real dreams? Dr Gastone Uguccioni, an Italian researcher, explained his childhood dreams at a conference in Rajasthan, India. He recalled seeing images of a structure that looked like a Hindu mandir, murti (statue of God) and items for puja (worship). He was bewildered by these dreams as such items of worship were not used in Italy and he had never seen a mandir during childhood. Therefore, it would have been difficult to comprehend why he was having such dreams. Science is unable to justify the reasons for Dr Uguccioni experiencing these dreams.

After seeing many images of similar mandirs, he concluded India was the land that had the answers to his dreams. Some may call it chance and luck which had first taken him to Chennai. He had then visited Mahabalipuram, which is not far from Chennai. He was shocked and amazed. He saw the same mandir and murti which he had seen in his dreams during childhood. Finally, he concluded his previous birth was in India and he was certain he was the pujari (priest). India is 3,287,590 km² in size; there are 29 states and approximately 1,609 cities. By chance it cannot be possible that Dr Gastone Uguccioni could end up finding the mandir that kept appearing in his dreams. This is the work of a deep karmic relationship. Ultimately it proves sometimes dreams are not simply dreams, but a message of deep value we simply cannot comprehend.

At the time of death

At the time of death one must have a very clear mind; what we think about at the time of death is what we receive. For example, if we think of our family, then it is very likely we will be reborn again into the same family.

There is a very well-known proverb of Jadbharat which we have already spoken about in the 'Reincarnation in the Shastras' section. Jadbharat, whilst on his penance, became attached to a fawn. Upon the time of his death he thought of this same fawn. As a result, he was born as a fawn in his next life. Due to his taap (penance), bhakti (devotion) and dedication to God in his life as a human, he was able to recollect his previous life when he was a fawn.

He had seen where he went wrong and was reborn as Jadbharat.

Ultimately, upon the time of death it is vital to remain clear minded and not think of our materialistic attachments, as this will only result in rebirth. We must focus on God and this will increase our chances of being one with God. Does one really want to be reborn and go through the struggles of life?

One may ask why most people do not remember their previous lives. It is by God's grace most people do not remember their previous lives. Think about it, if you remembered all of the pain and suffering you went through in each lifetime, would you be able to live a peaceful life? Human beings struggle to live a peaceful life with just the present life's pain and suffering. Therefore, coping with previous lives' pain and suffering is out of the question.

Is our fate predetermined or do we make our own decisions?

This is one of humankind's most common questions, and the answer to this question is simple. We as humans like to be in control—when we are not in control, we are vulnerable and this worries us. Fate is determined from our previous actions and even actions from previous lives. This links with karma. The actions we carry out affect our future. For example, if we carry out a good act such as, helping someone in need, then we shall receive good karma which will be a good outcome. If we carry out a bad act such as, intentionally wishing bad upon an individual, then we shall receive bad karma which will be a bad outcome.

As I mentioned earlier, the fruits of our actions may not be reaped straight away and may be reaped later on in life or even in another life. This being said, the fruits of our actions can also be reaped immediately. Our previous actions will determine aspects of our lives and certain activities in our life will happen, but we still always have a choice.

One of these choices is how to understand what has happened and respond accordingly. It is necessary to understand that we may have done something or carried out an action to cause certain events to occur; for example, if you have murdered someone, the result of that will lead to prosecution and being sentenced to prison. This is the outcome of your actions and you must accept and understand this. Conversely, one has the option to not understand and retaliate in a way that causes more harm. Going back to the example of murdering someone, you could lie about the murder, attempt to flee the country, or do something else in anger such as hurt someone else. All of these would amount in bad karma.

We also have a choice in what to do with our present life and what actions we choose to carry out. We must understand how these actions could impact our present life. For example, if you own a shop you can make the choice of opening the shop and working a full day, but how many customers you will get is not up to you—that is up to the grace of God.

It is up to us as individuals what actions we take and as a result what karma we receive in return. Ultimately one should always think about this when deciding on their actions.

What is heaven and what is hell?

From a young age children are often told to behave and live a good life as only then can they go to heaven, and if one has lived a bad life full of sin, then they obtain the displeasure of hell.

Is heaven a place above the sky in some place where everything is calm, peaceful, joyful and everything is perfect and everything falls into place?

Is hell a place which causes so much displeasure that it is a fate worse than death?

Heaven and hell are like gateways into religion. Human nature ultimately seeks the path to heaven due to the experience of bliss and happiness and not hell due to fear and potential pain. The idea of heaven gives humankind an aim to work towards, without which they would walk away from the path of righteousness.

However, once an individual meets a sat guru they are enlightened as to what heaven and hell truly are. The sat guru is the initial medium between the individual and God who enables the individual to understand what God is. It is also the sat guru who allows the individual to make a connection with the Paramatma which resides within them. Once an individual has realised the purpose of life by the knowledge gained from their sat guru, they are at one with God. This is true heaven. The individual experiences satisfaction and peace like no other feeling. Heaven is not a place in the sky; heaven is being one with God in this lifetime and after this life. Hell is a life of an individual who has not experienced this bliss, one who is unable to obtain knowledge, one who is knowledgeable but does not act upon it or one who cannot walk on the path of righteousness.

It is like when a child drinks powdered milk from a bottle— the child is content and happy for a while, but eventually the child will throw away the bottle and want to have its mother's organic milk. This illustrates how the child goes back to the fundamentals, the core, the meaningful aspects. In the same respect, an individual will be happy and content with working towards attaining a place in heaven, which is deemed to be some place in the sky. However, there will come a point in time where this individual is not content with this theory and will question: What is religion? What is heaven and hell? This is when the need for a sat guru will arise.

The sat guru is able to assist the individual on the true meanings of life and the path towards true heaven.

Many people may claim to be one with God, but how many people are really at one with God? There are seven energy points (chakras), and the highest one is at the top of a human being's forehead. This knowledge can also be found in Buddhism and also the art of yoga. When concentrating on God and the position of the seventh chakra whilst meditating, you can feel the presence of your highest chakra as it tingles. This is when you are at one with God. This is heaven and this is when you see the world and all aspects of the world and life for what they truly are.

Chapter 5- Religion with Science

How were humans ever created?

Some may ask what the purpose of creating humans was. It is a simple explanation in fact. We only see it in films, animations or cartoons where a power so great thinks of an object or a creation and it appears out of thin air. It does not mean to say science does not exist; it does. Pramukh Swami Maharaj of the BAPS Swaminarayan Sanstha has a very good proverb which describes religion and science very well. Religion is like a car and the headlights are like science. The headlights show the way and explain aspects only to a certain degree. Thereafter religion comes into play.

In this instance God simply thought about creating a world, a solar system, a Milky Way, a whole universe for creations to admire the beauty, peace and tranquility of the world. One of those creations is now known as humans. Many other creations such as fish, animals, birds, insects, trees and so on were created. This includes dinosaurs and the first human beings ever to be created.

This defies the scientific theory of the 'Big Bang', which is the most common theory of how the universe began. One theory is by Edwin Hubble. Edwin Hubble made some of the most important discoveries in modern astronomy. Such discoveries resulted in the world's most powerful telescope being named after him. In 1929 a discovery by Edwin Hubble stated that galaxies outside our own Milky Way were all moving away from us, each at a speed proportional to its distance from Earth. He came to the conclusion that this meant that there must have been a time (now known to be about 14 billion years ago) when the entire universe was contained in a single point in space. Due to all of the energy and mass in one space, a huge explosion took place (the Big Bang). However, there are facts that science cannot answer. Scientists can only speculate how life began on Earth but do not actually have an answer.

Living beings are unique in the way they store and process information. Cells read, interpret and carry out instructions carried in their genetic code. But the theory of evolution cannot explain the source of the information. So where does this information come from?

Furthermore, protein molecules are necessary for the functioning of a cell. A typical protein molecule consists of hundreds of amino acids strung together in a specific sequence. Additionally, the protein molecule must fold into a specific three-dimensional shape for it to function. Some scientists conclude the odds of one protein molecule forming spontaneously are extremely unlikely. Renowned physicist Paul Davies states since a functioning cell requires thousands of different proteins, it is not credible to suppose they formed by chance alone.

Cells within the body perform extraordinary tasks such as transporting and converting nutrients into energy, repairing the cell and conveying all other sorts of messages throughout the cell. Can random mutations and natural selection really be responsible for such sophistication?

Animals and humans develop from a single fertilised egg. Inside the embryo (fertilised egg) the cells multiply and specialise to eventually form parts of the body. How does each cell know how to function, where to go and what to become? Evolution cannot explain this.

Human beings are conscious and self-aware; they have the ability to reason and think, and possess moral qualities such as generosity and a sense of right and wrong. Evolution cannot explain the existence of such unique qualities of human beings.

Michael Behe, a professor of biological sciences, states all of the facts above point to a higher power responsible for the creations we see. Mere luck, chance and random mutations cannot result in such sophistication.

It is difficult to imagine the world being cruel at the time when God created it. When it was first created there was harmony, peace and tranquility. There are four yugs (times of the earth) which vary in characteristics. In order of occurrence these are: Satya Yug, Treta Yug, Dwapar Yug and Kali Yug. A point to consider is that the length of each yug is calculated using ancient astronomy as instructed per Vedic scriptures. However, the overall length of each yug varies slightly according to who completed the calculation due to the complexity of the calculation. Despite these slight variances, all Hinduism academics agree that we are currently in Kali Yug, and the end of the Mahabharat dictated this just over 5,000 years ago.

Humankind was more powerful in the earlier yugs and lived to an older age, i.e. thousands of years old. *How is this possible?* you may ask. *Could this really have happened?*

In earlier yugs humans had stronger minds and willpower due to concentration on God, meditation and yoga. Humans in earlier yugs were much purer and realised the presence of God, resulting in them focusing much of their time connecting with God through meditation and yoga. Through this they had exceptional mind control, enabling them to have unique and special powers. For example, this is how the likes of Ram Bhagwan, Krishna Bhagwan,

Arjun and all other gods and godlike beings obtained their powers. Yoga helps strengthen one's mind and provides impeccable mind strength, thus yoga and meditation go hand in hand. The art of meditation and yoga gives way to the phrase: 'The mind will achieve what the body cannot'.

Satya Yug was the golden age. During this yug all living beings lived in peace and harmony. There was no such thing as evil as all was pure. There were no killings, no rape, and no sinful acts. As each yug passed humankind changed for the worse. They slowly forgot their connection with God and spirituality, important lessons learnt by forefathers were not passed down from generation to generation, and traditions and culture were less prevalent. This corrupted their minds for desires of little importance such as wealth, power, lust and so on.

After Satya Yug came the Treta Yug, Dwapar Yug, and finally Kali Yug. The lifespan and unique powers of human beings in earlier yugs were also much longer and more prevalent due to their spirituality, mind control, focus on yoga and focus on God. As each yug passed, the lifespan and the number of people having unique abilities decreased.

Controlling one's mind is the most difficult task in the whole of the universe. You may have experienced this many times. If not, try it now—attempt focusing on nothing but God or a being that is important to you for only 2 minutes. If your thought changes even for one second, you have lost. Consequently, imagine the strength of a certain individual's mind control by being able to focus on God for extended periods of time. How is it people are able to do this?

Previously, many thousands of years ago, human beings had better mind control due to special mantras, focus on religion and God, and a strong focus on yoga. I must emphasise how important yoga is for spiritual development. Individuals today think yoga is only a form of physical fitness; however, it is also for mental fitness and spiritual wellbeing. Even in ancient scriptures of Hinduism the importance and benefits of yoga are emphasised. Yoga not only helps bring more oxygen to the brain for us to function more effectively and feel less tired but also helps unlock our inner self. In chapter 4 we spoke about becoming one with God through our seventh chakra. The principle of the seven chakras (7 energy points in our body) also applies to the principles of yoga. The purpose of yoga and meditation is to help you to unlock your seventh chakra (the highest chakra).

The quality of the food we eat today is also a factor we must consider. The food that humans would have consumed many centuries ago was natural and organic, thus beneficial for our body. Since then genetically modified crops are commonly used. The food we eat in today's world has been injected with many different drugs to create abnormal growth. This results in a reduction of vitamins and minerals, and the food does not benefit the human body as it once did. This negatively impacts our mind, body and spirit.

To put the power of yoga into perspective, let us take an example of an individual attempting to give up smoking. The individual would find this a huge task as it has become a norm in their daily life. However, if they incorporated yoga and meditation into their daily life, they would feel the ability to control their mind grow over time, resulting in increases in their willpower. They will be able to control these cravings and eventually give up. The benefits of yoga and meditation are proven and should be practiced.

We have all heard stories or know someone who supposedly has some unique powers such as seeing into the future, being able to see spirits, being able to contact spirits and so forth. A question arises in most people's minds as to whether or not this is true. Can this really happen? Many people doubt, question and do not believe in this, and to a certain degree rightly so.

However, the fact of the matter is there are individuals with certain special capabilities. Humans many years ago and in ancient times were able to control their minds effectively due to yoga. As a result of this control, they were able to obtain special powers such as seeing into the future.

There are very few people in this world today who truly have these sorts of powers. This comes down to their karma, the fruits of their karma from previous births, and the existing birth and the ability to control their mind. Each individual has their own karma and consequences of their karma, and very few people have the ability to actually fully control their mind. It truly is unique and remarkable when an individual actually has such powers.

An excellent example to understand yoga and mind control can be provided by Swami Vivekananda and Baba Ramdev. Swami Vivekananda lived a very short but successful life during the years of 1863 to 1902. It was filled with immense labour and achievement. Swami Vivekananda had many questions about the world, religion and God and had found himself a guru who could answer these questions for him. Guru Sri Ramakrishna became his guru and taught him the righteous path, imparted knowledge, gave him an understanding of God where he could feel God's presence, and transformed him into a sage and prophet with the authority to teach. After the death of Guru Sri Ramkrishna, Swami Vivekananda wandered India and other countries abroad teaching what he had learnt.

There is a very well-known story about the power of yoga that Swami Vivekananda experienced and discussed in his book *Powers of the Mind*. Swami Vivekananda had heard about a man who would immediately answer the questions of people who went near him. In addition, he had also heard that this man could foretell the future. Swami Vivekananda had gone with a few friends with a question each in their mind to see this man. As soon as the man saw one of them, he repeated their questions and gave the answers to them. He then wrote something on paper for each individual and folded this up and asked each individual to sign the paper and to keep it in their pocket until he asked for it again. He then told each of the individuals of some events that would happen to them in the future.

Next he told them to think of a word or sentence in any language. Swami Vivekananda thought of a long sentence from Sanskrit, a language the man had no knowledge of. He then instructed Swami Vivekananda to take out the signed piece of paper and read it. Astounded, he read what was written before him. It was the sentence he was thinking of in his head, except this was written on the paper an hour ago.

One of Swami Vivekananda's friends thought of a sentence in Arabic from the Quran. The likelihood of the man getting this correct was still less possible. However, when he had opened his piece of paper, it was the sentence he was thinking of. Another one of his friends was a physician. He thought of a sentence from a German medical book, and again this sentence was written on the piece of paper. All were astounded by this man's abilities.

Swami Vivekananda had gone again a few days later with a different group of friends, and again the man came out triumphant.

How is it possible that this man was able to do such wonderful things, you may ask. Yoga and meditation is the answer—the ability to control one's mind. There are not many people left in the world who are able to control their mind in this manner, but they do exist in all countries. There are many people in the world who imitate such powers and con the public. But what are they imitating? There must be truth somewhere in such acts for this to be called imitation.

Let us put this into context to help your understanding. The body is the grossest part (the biggest part). We can narrow the body down into finer and finer movements. The finest part we call the soul. We also know the power is in the fine movements. For example, when a person picks up a weight, we see their muscles swell with signs of exertion. We think the muscles are the powerful entities and often people ask how big are your muscles, arms, legs etc. Ironically, it is the thin thread-like nerves that bring power to muscles. As soon as these threads are cut off from reaching the muscles, the muscles will no longer work despite how big they are. These nerves are powered by something finer, and that again is powered by something finer and so on. When movement occurs in the grossest part, we see it and thus recognise it. But when movement occurs in the finer parts, we do not see that.

In the same way that plants grow by watering them, humans grow when they attain the power to control their minds through yoga, meditation and self-realisation.

Controlling one's mind is no easy task. It takes years upon years of practice to obtain perfection. However, every time you try you will improve. Swami Vivekananda describes obtaining mind control as being harder than running your own business. The people that obtained such unique powers focused, meditated, and practiced for hours upon hours in a day. It is like with anything—the more you practice, the longer you practice, the harder you practice, the better you become.

Sciences had originated from the great country of India. They knew about mathematics and were the first to use the numerical values 1,2,3,4, etc. after Sanskrit. Ingredients that doctors put in modern day medicines such as ginger were used as medicines thousands of years ago. Plastic surgery originated from India thousands of years before the world had even heard of it. The laws of gravitation were known in India thousands of years before Sir Isaac Newton's birth. In addition to these great discoveries, thousands of years ago rishimunis and yogis (sages) had mastered mind control and showed us what was possible with it. The powers of mind control are phenomenal.

Additionally, strong mind control and yoga also prolong life. It not only entails spirituality but also is heavily linked to science. Baba Ramdev is a well-known spiritual and inspirational guru who specialises in ayurvedic medicine and yoga. He has been working for the greater good of mankind, especially in India. Baba Ramdev is particularly well-known for his work against corruption in India as well as his work concerning the disastrous effects of using ferris fertilisers and pesticides and the current state of poverty.

Ramdev was born as Ramkrishna Yadav to Ram Nivas Yadav and Gulabo Devi in the Alipur village of the Mahendragarh district in the Haryana state of India. He had a formal education until 8th standard in school. He then studied Indian scripture, yoga and Sanskrit in various gurukuls (schools). He became a sanyasi (a saint) and eventually was called by his popular name "Baba Ramdev". He is well-known for providing free yoga exercises, hints, tips and guides for everyone.

A student studying in the Indian Institute of Technology Kharagpur was diagnosed with liver and pancreatic cancer. His tumour was 8kg in weight when he had found out. He decided not to use chemotherapy or any other modern day conventional drug or therapy. He had simply done a yogic breathing exercise all day called pranayam. Doing this simple breathing exercise cured his cancer. Modern day therapy would have provided small chances of him living (in the case of this student, 10-20%); however, a simple yoga breathing exercise was able to kill this cancer. Some may call this a miracle, but this is simply the benefits of yoga, which were written in the Vedic scriptures thousands and thousands of years ago.

The organisation Cancer Research recognises the importance of yoga and its wonders and even dedicates a section of their website for this. The website states, "Yoga teachers promote yoga as a way of staying healthy and preventing illness. If you use the correct yogic breathing techniques, the postures will stimulate your nervous system, make your muscles and joints more flexible, and relax your mind and body. The exercises and breathing improve your oxygen and blood supply. In turn, this helps your circulation and breathing, which promotes general good health."

Chapter 6- Hindu Gods, Mandir and Prayer

Who is the Supreme God?

Who the Supreme God is in Hinduism is the ultimate question for many Hindus. There are many subsections within Hinduism that have their own view with regards to behaving and believing. For example, there are Hindus who worship solely one idol/God; there are Hindus who worship only their Kurdevi (family goddess – explained further in chapter 6); and there are different subsets of Hinduism such as Hare Krishna, Swaminarayan, Vaishnavism, Shaivism and so forth, and all these different types of Hindus will have slightly different ways of thinking and doing things.

In addition, there are many stories and illustrations about various Hindu gods which display their valour, greatness and godly qualities. For example, Shankar Bhagwan, Krishna Bhagwan, Hanuman Bhagwan, Ram Bhagwan, Vishnu Bhagwan, Parvati Maa, Amba Maa, Durga Maa and so on. How does one decide which God to follow and worship?

Let us break this down and start from the beginning. Despite which sector of Hinduism an individual follows, they all have one thing in common. They all understand and believe the concept of Paramatma, the Supreme God being in all living things. For example, trees, animals, insects, including humans and all other living beings, contain Paramatma in them. This fact is repeated time and time again in all the religious scriptures and all big events that have defined Hinduism such as the Mahabharat and Ramayan. Not only this, this fact is also conceived in all other religions too but is just called different names; for example, Christianity, Islam and Judaism call it the Holy Spirit. Sikhism and Jainism also call it Paramatma, and Buddhism also believes in this concept as this is how enlightenment is obtained.

If the Supreme God, Paramatma, exists in all living beings, it would be wise to focus on this rather than what people speculate to be Supreme Gods, gods and demigods. Of course this is the rationale one should take. By worshipping Paramatma you are worshipping all gods at the same time, as even the things you perceive to be God have Paramatma in them; for example, Krishna Bhagwan, Ram Bhagwan, Shankar Bhagwan, etc. all have Paramatma in them.

These figures that Hindus class as gods are in fact humans but enlightened souls, which means they were one with God, making them godlike. As they were enlightened souls, they were pure, righteous and acted for the good.

Also, as they were enlightened, they were able to do things normal humans could not—they had special powers and godly qualities. In fact, it was humans that made them gods because they were superior to us. They were worth worshiping and idolising, but they also had to attain enlightenment to reach that status. However, it is crucial to remember they were god-like and not in fact God. In addition, people worshipped them more once their bodies had perished and passed on. It is like with all great beings once they have passed away—their work becomes exemplary, and they are praised.

To take this into consideration, let us think of an example. When Mahatma Gandhi was alive, he did great things for the world and India. He had created equality and peace and abolished the British rule in India. As a result, not only citizens of India but also people from all over the world loved, cherished and praised Mahatma Gandhi. People bowed down before him, respected him greatly, and treated him like a god. After he passed away, people started to worship him and make statues in remembrance of him. They treated him like a god. This is similar to how the Hindu gods such as Krishna Bhagwan and Ram Bhagwan attained their superior status as gods.

The likes of Krishna Bhagwan and Ram Bhagwan also had gurus to guide them. If they were supreme since birth, then why would they need gurus?

In the Mahabharat (2014 episodes on television) when Krishna Bhagwan is explaining to Arjun who he truly is, he says to him, "I am God, but even you can be God Arjun and so can everyone else." This is a pivotal point most people miss out on. He then goes on to say how God (Paramatma) is in all living things. Krishna Bhagwan beautifully illustrates how everyone can be one with God and be godlike using the following example: When a raindrop from the sky falls and meets the ocean, it does not remain as a raindrop; instead it becomes the ocean. In the same respect when an individual becomes enlightened and self-realised, they are at one with God, making them godlike.

After knowing this truth one shall realise what is a Supreme God. However, it is crucial to remember this is not to say to disrespect other gods, gurus or godlike figures, for there are many things we can also learn from them. From being one with Paramatma, the Supreme God, we also worship all other gods or forms of God.

In reality there is only one God. Some call this God Allah, some call it Jesus, some call it Krishna Bhagwan, some simply call it God. As stated earlier in this chapter, the concept of Paramatma is believed widely in many major religions, however is simply called different names.

If most major religions point to this fact, there must be truth in it, but not only this—it can be proven. There are three main energy points (seven in total) within our body where our chakras (spiritual energy) are stored. The places where this spiritual energy is present is also where Paramatma resides. The first main one is near the abdomen (where the belly button is), the second one is where the heart is and the third is at the top of the forehead. As mentioned earlier, the highest chakra in our body is the seventh chakra. This concept is also widely believed by those practicing yoga and Buddhism. When meditating or chanting God's name, concentration is placed upon the seventh chakra; you can feel the spiritual energy within you, you can see things clearer and you can feel bliss.

There are also special maha mantras (great mantras) that can be obtained that help you become one with God. When saying these mantras, you can feel a tingling vibration where the highest chakra is. Not many people in this world are able to do this. As time has passed the unique people who hold key knowledge like this have decreased throughout the yugs.

There are gurus who can give mantras, but not all these mantras are powerful, real or do anything. Finding a real guru who can help you attain self-realisation is extremely difficult. Thus those who obtain this knowledge are extremely fortunate.

In reality there are no differences between Hindus, Christians, Muslims, Jews, and so on. We all bleed red blood, we all breathe the same air, we are all made from the same compositions of elements, we all have Paramatma in all of us, and in reality we are all one. We should not discriminate against one another based on religion, skin colour, or ethnicity as this is wrong.

So why do different religions exist you may ask? Different religions exist due to the culture of the country you are raised in. All religions at their roots are peaceful, have an emphasis on equality of all living beings, and focus on spirituality. It is human beings that have changed, altered and tailored spirituality and religion over the past yugs to fit what we want and our lifestyles.

What is a Kur Devi?

The term Kur Devi refers to a family's goddess that has been worshipped over previous generations dating hundreds, if not thousands, of years ago. The family will hold a special connection to the Kur Devi and vice versa. For example, one family's Kur Devi could be Amba Maa and another's could be Durga Maa (these are different types of goddesses). As per family tradition, their Kur Devi is paid the upmost respect as it is this goddess the family turns to in a time of need. Often a person would do a special prayer, katha (religious discussion) or a havan (sacred ceremony involving fire) where women or girls are invited and they all eat prashad (food blessed by God) together after. This process is called a goyni and is done especially for the Kur Devi of the person hosting the event. The food is offered first to the Kur Devi and only then can the rest eat.

Kur Devi literally translates to the wording 'mother goddess'. This being said, our own mothers can be regarded as a Kur Devi. They gave birth to us and tend to nurture us, help us grow, provide us with love and care, and help us with our problems throughout our lifetime.

It is not wrong to worship your family Kur Devi as it is never incorrect to worship God. However, is following traditions made by our previous generations correct? We should think about the reasoning as to why we carry out activities sometimes and not simply blindly just follow them. This is not to say we should not carry out these activities; it is saying we should still carry out these activities but also concentrate on what we need to do, and that is to learn our purpose of life. The purpose of our life is to realise who and what God is and what we truly are. By understanding the Paramatma in us and establishing a connection, we automatically have worshipped the

Supreme God, which covers all gods and goddesses, including Kur Devis.

How can two individuals who are from the same entity be living at the same time, e.g. Bhagwan Parshuram and Ram Bhagwan?

In the text below, Vishnu Bhagwan (God Vishnu) and Bhagwan Parshuram (God Parshuram) will be described. Ram Bhagwan, Hanuman Bhagwan, Shankar Bhagwan have previously been referred to and described in this book.

In Hinduism there is a Tri-murti of Supreme Gods (3 Supreme Gods). Vishnu Bhagwan is the preserver of the universes. He is the god that reincarnates when the world needs to be educated upon righteousness again. Bhagwan Parshuram is Vishnu Bhagwan's 6th avatar (reincarnation).

There may have been many cases where reincarnations of a god have existed at the same time, for example Ram Bhagwan and Bhagwan Parshuram, Shankar Bhagwan and Hanuman Bhagwan.

Ram Bhagwan and Bhagwan Parshuram are reincarnations of Vishnu Bhagwan (The preserver god). Shankar Bhagwan is a part of Hanuman Bhagwan (Shankar Bhagwan was not reincarnated as Hanuman Bhagwan but was a part of Hanuman Bhagwan). Immediately the question may arise as to how a god can be a reincarnation/a part of another being if their old form is still existent. From what we know, a god comes down in a time of need when righteousness and religion's concepts seem obscure to teach us the ways of a virtuous life once more. Once the god's work is done, they leave Earth. Therefore, how is this possible?

Everything in this world is created by God, including humans, trees, animals, insects, the planets, stars and so forth, thus giving way to the explanation God is existent in all creations. Many times in major religious battles this fact has been repeated time and time again, for example in the Ramayan and the Mahabharat. In the Mahabharat, Krishna Bhagwan said if you placed the point of a needle anywhere in the universe then even there, God is present. There is no place in the universe where God is not present.

If God is everywhere (in every single human, plant, animal, insect, etc.) then God is already in many different forms. Then why cannot God be in two different reincarnations?

Why do we go Mandir?

Firstly, mandirs are man-made objects and are not created by God or even requested to be built by God. Hindus have created them as a place for people to come to worship God. This being said, personal mandirs can also be made to have in houses. Also, inside mandirs you have murtis (statues of God) to worship. These murtis are used as a medium to connect with God. Priests carry out a yagna (ritual) before installing a murti in a mandir. This yagna is to call God into the murti. Through the murti people feel they can connect with God.

Without a medium, it is extremely difficult for one to connect with God, and the one that can connect with God without a medium is on the way to true self-realisation. An individual can be taught to worship Paramatma within them. Consequently, this means an individual can connect with God without the use of a murti. However, this is an extremely difficult task and few people are able to do so. As a result, people tend to use a murti as a medium as a means of worshipping god.

The question then arises: Does praying to a murti really help? Does the murti really listen to what you are saying and talk back? The answer for different people will vary, but in reality praying to a murti does not truly help as the murti cannot talk back to you. Attending mandir is a positive activity, but this is merely the first step into your spiritual journey. There is much more depth behind religion and spirituality; therefore, you should yearn to further develop your knowledge. Conversely, concentrating your efforts on being one with the Paramatma would be much more beneficial, but this is also much harder. You will be able to feel the presence of the Paramatma in you and have clarity of what is wrong and what is right and what life is. How to live life will become clearer over time.

Meditation is key to solving all problems. Meditating upon Paramatma at a time of crisis will show the path you seek and can be used as a form of prayer. However, this being said, it cannot and should not only be used at the time of a crisis, but should be practiced throughout daily life. This would improve aspects of one's life greatly. The individual will feel a closer connection with God; they will feel more positive and have more focus. They would be more satisfied and content with life, and the aims and objectives of what they want to achieve will become distinct. Ultimately they will know how to proceed to the next step of self-realisation.

Why is it not correct to only pray to God in a time of need?

People always remember God in a time of need; for example, when something bad happens people will remember God and say 'oh God please help me'. People even say God's name when frustrated, shocked or in awe without realising and given what context it is in, it can again also be illustrated as a sign for help. For example, it is common for people to say 'for God's sake' when frustration occurs and 'oh my God' when in shock or awe.

Some individuals pray to God, and when they do not get what they prayed for they say, "What is the purpose of praying to God if you cannot get what you want?" Let us think about this logically. Does it make sense to get what you pray for if you only remember God at a time of need? No, it does not. One should remember God throughout their whole life, every day as much as possible.

When individuals normally pray to God they most likely pray for themselves. For example, "Oh God, please help me pass my exams. If I pass my exams, then I will offer flowers at the mandir every day for one week." If an individual only prays in a time of need and prays for themselves for selfish motives, how can they expect their prayers to be heard?

Even if an individual remembers God on a regular basis and prays every day, it does not mean all of their prayers will be answered. It is not as simple as that. There are other factors that come into play such as karma and the consequences of karma, although we may never know exactly how the action of karma has impacted us due to the complex fabrications of karma. We shall use the example of an individual praying to pass their exams again. This individual may not pass their exams to be a doctor regardless of how hard they worked, revised and attempted to pass these exams. The rationale behind this is maybe they were never meant to be a doctor. Rather they were meant to proceed into the field of engineering for some unknown reason. There would be a link to karma. Maybe in a previous life all they wanted to do was become an engineer, and in this life they finally got the chance to do so.

The reasoning may not be clear at the time, but there is a possibility of finding out what it may be. A priest or individual with the genuine ability to look at horoscopes and star signs may be able to provide reasoning; however, these abilities are rare and finding someone who can successfully do this is difficult.

When an individual prays they should attempt to pray for the strength to live a good and honest life, for God to give them the knowledge and ability to become self-realised and the compassion to serve and help others to make the world a better place, and not just for materialistic objects. They should pray for the welfare of the world and not just their own personal welfare.

Touching on this, in the same respect when giving blessings to someone, an individual normally says, "May you have a good job, be wealthy, have a good wife/husband," and so on. Rather than bless people with these materialistic desires, you should bless them to be knowledgeable, be successful in their spiritual life or live a good life.

What is the purpose of fasting?

Fasting is a concept that many Hindis follow. Some carry out the act of fasting as they wish to fast, some will carry out the act of fasting as they are advised to do it, and some carry out the act of fasting simply because other people they know also carry out the act of fasting.

There is nothing wrong in any of the above reasons, but it must be understood what exactly this act of fasting achieves.

Firstly, we must understand the act of fasting is not a necessity. You do not have to fast and it is optional. Taking this into consideration, one should not fast if they are unwell or have health problems and need to eat, and one should not make themselves ill by fasting.

When you fast it is seen as religious and holy. Therefore, you are consciously observing your behaviour and avoiding committing any unholy (i.e., sinful) acts. As a result, you obtain fewer pap karmas (bad karma). Instead, what the individual fasting concentrates on is carrying out good deeds to obtain punya karmas (good karma). They do this by helping others (charitable work), giving donations, focusing more time on God, and spending more time worshiping God. In respect to the points above, fasting is very good for the individual observing the fast. This is the main benefit and purpose of fasting.

Ironically, these are actions an individual should be doing regardless. The concept of fasting simply motivates them and provides the individual with an opportunity to carry out the actions they should be carrying out.

Let us take an example of a yogi (also known as sanyasi and sadhu (saint)). A yogi is one who abandons the world and seeks solitude in remote locations to mediate and become one with God. (Note: not all yogis/sanyasis/sadhus seek solitude in remote locations, although it is common amongst many.)

Whilst they meditate and build their mind power/control, they are able to control their senses better. They will find they will not be as hungry and will only consume what the body needs, which can be considerably less than what you eat on a day-to-day basis. Therefore, can this be seen as a type of fasting? Yes, it can and the benefits are you only eat what the body needs and therefore are not materialistically attached to food. Of course only eating what your body requires is promoting good health. You may question: How can one be materialistically attached to food? When we crave certain types of food and we must have that food, this is classed as being materialistically attached to food.

Further to this point, there are ironically and conveniently many different types of fasting in Hinduism. There is a type of fast where only water can be consumed and a type of fast where only fruit can be consumed. There is also a type of fast where you can only eat one proper meal in the day but still eat certain foods and fruits during the day (ektano)—however, this food should not contain onions and garlic. Onions and garlic are considered to be Tamas foods (foods which negatively affect the body), and the food is initially offered to God first. Therefore, the food cannot contain onions or garlic.

It is also a common practise amongst many sects within Hinduism such as Hare Krishna and Swaminarayan, and Jainism. Generally, these fasts involve eating simpler foods such as fruits and grains, which are beneficial for the body as such food provides essential nutrients and is much easier for the body to digest. One may question why different types of fasting exist. It is so people can pick what is most convenient for them. This illustrates how this concept was created by humankind.

In addition there are many holy days and months throughout the year such as Ekadashi (the 11th day of each half of the month in the Vedic lunar calendar where fasting is observed for Krishna Bhagwan), Shravan Mayno (the month where the churning of oceans took place, releasing a poison that had to be consumed by Lord Shiva, which he stored it in his throat, subsequently turning his throat blue), Parsotam Mayno (when the lunar calendar adds one extra month every third year during which fasting and charitable acts are believed to be very fruitful), fasting on Mondays for Shankar Bhagwan, and fasting on Saturdays for Hanuman Bhagwan. Shravan Mayno is seen as the most religious month in Hinduism to fast, donate money, participate in charity work and so on. But why is this the case?

The truth of the matter is Shravan mayno, along with all other holy days, is no more important than normal days. You will not receive any greater benefit by carrying out fasting or other pious acts on holy days as opposed to non-religious days. These religious days merely provide further motivation to individuals to think about their actions and consequences.

Why is it when females are ovulating they cannot go to the mandir or participate in religious activities?

There are many speculations about traditions, but one of the traditions that is most speculated about is women not being able to go to the mandir or take part in religious activities when they are ovulating. It is believed that during this time they are impure and therefore cannot visit the mandir or take part in religious activities. In some cases individuals keep their towels and toiletries separate from others and attempt to only sit in one spot. They do this to ensure that they do not make everything else around them impure. However, for hygiene reasons having separate towels may seem justifiable. In other cases some individuals take it to the extent where they do not even pray or they feel guilty worshipping God; however, this could not be further from the truth.

Many thousands of years ago women who were ovulating were kept away from doing work to allow them to rest. Historically women worked extremely hard not just in the house but also out of the house, especially at mandirs, with tasks such as cooking and cleaning. This is the reason why historically women who were ovulating did not go to the mandir or partake in religious activities. Society today has extracted this and warped it into something which is far from the truth. If a woman is ovulating it does not make them impure and they do not have to separate themselves from others by sitting in one place. They can still go to mandir and they most definitely can engage in religious activities.

This relates to the point I made earlier: The Supreme God, Paramatma, is in everything and every living being, including women. Does this mean God cannot reside in women when they are ovulating as they are 'impure'? Of course not—Paramatma does not leave the body of a woman if they are ovulating. In fact, Paramatma stays within them at all times, and therefore women cannot be impure during this time.

If one looks deeper into these 'traditions', what you will tend to find is there was logical and rational reasoning as to why society took the actions they did. However, in today's age, society now has transformed these actions into ridiculous superstitions. For example, there is a common superstition amongst the Indian society in particular where you should not cut your nails at nighttime; otherwise they go into the mouths of your ancestors. The real reason for this is because people used to cut their nails at night and traditionally threw them outside. Therefore, in the morning birds would see these nails as rice and eat them, and as a result eventually die.

There is another tradition where people cannot cut their nails near the time of a funeral. Again there is logic and a rationale behind this. Historically people would have done this to ensure they do not cut into their skin as they cut their nails because during the final ritual of a deceased when you say your final goodbye, germs, bacteria and disease could easily come into your body through the broken skin.

There are many traditions like this. What we must learn is to filter the traditions from religious traditions as this is where confusion occurs and questions arise. The traditions named above are not religious traditions. With this in mind, think about the difference between traditions and religious traditions.

Why do we go on a pilgrimage?

Pilgrimage is the word for going on a trip to a place of religious significance. People go on pilgrimages as they wish to be in the place God was in. They wish to walk those very grounds and stand in that exact spot. People want to visit all of these places where the stories of God took place, for example Kuruksetra where the battle of the Mahabharat took place, Dwarka where Krishna Bhagwan resided, the 12 temples which are built next to the 12 shivlings (these places signify where Shankar Bhagwan appeared), and so on.

People do this for various reasons, to build a closer connection with God, to worship and obtain blessings, or to simply see the place where gods have been as they have an interest.

Most people go on pilgrimages to worship and be blessed in the area where God resided. They believe it will hold more significance and be a blessing of greater power. They save up money, take holiday from school/work and put in a great amount of effort. The question that arises is: What does one truly gain from going on a pilgrimage?

There should really only be two reasons why you should go on a pilgrimage—if it is for a particular reason, for example, you said you will go if you pass your exams, etc., and if you have an interest in such places. Although most people go because God resided there and they go to seek blessings, this should not be one of the reasons you should go on a pilgrimage.

Why is this, you may be thinking. God was present in these places of pilgrimage; however, God is also present in all living beings. If one wants to simply go on a pilgrimage because God resided there, they do not have to leave their house, for God is also present within them. They can obtain the blessings they seek by meditating upon the God within them. As a result of this, they will realise what they truly are (a soul), what the purpose of their life is, and what they want to achieve, and they will eradicate all of their bad qualities. What blessing can be greater? They are closer to becoming an enlightened individual, thus leading to true peacefulness and happiness.

Chapter 7- Marriage

How was the concept of marriage created?

There was no tradition of marriage before many yugs ago when mankind was first created. The concept of marriage did not exist. Individuals would engage in sexual intercourse with one another without thinking about the consequences and depart on their separate paths. As a result, women were left to deal with the after effects of giving birth and bringing up a child alone. Eventually, humankind realised how wrong this was and how difficult one's life becomes by living in such a way. Consequently, the concept of marriage was created. This meant individuals could not simply engage in sexual intercourse and depart on their separate paths; they had to be committed, understanding and compassionate and build a life with their chosen partners.

Is it correct to have several partners, in particular several wives?

It is important to know the difference between traditions we have made and traditions that have been passed down from God. This section focuses on a tradition that is man-made. Before, thousands and thousands of years ago, some kings and common people had several wives as they had an abundance of money and thought they could do anything they wished if they had money. Money was seen to be a power. It might seem morally wrong in today's society, but is having several wives or partners a sin?

It is not a sin if a woman chooses to marry a king or a common man knowing they are already married. It is only wrong if the woman is being forced to marry someone they do not wish to.

In the same respect, it is not wrong for women to have more than one husband as long as the men are not forced to marry her. It is important to remember men and women are equals and should not be discriminated against one another. There are many in today's society who do not understand this and think men are supreme compared to women. People who have this thought process generally believe men should not bow down to women.

There are two points in relation to this. Firstly, Krishna Bhagwan used to bow down to his wives as a sign of respect every day. If such a pious, virtuous and pure themen in today's world not? Why is it we do not comprehend this message? This does not explicitly mean you have to bow down to women, but you must at the very least respect them. Secondly, there are sub-sections within Hinduism and individuals who bow down and touch other people's feet as a form of greeting. To one who has not seen this it would seem extremely unusual, and they may think, *Why is this person touching my feet?* However, what they are doing is respecting the Paramatma that resides in every being, be it either man or woman. These two points clearly demonstrate the importance of equality amongst genders and respecting both men and women.

This being said, one should only ever have more than one partner if they can treat each partner equally in terms of love and affection. If they cannot, then they should not have more than one partner as this would not be fair and just.

In today's world, generally the practice of having several partners has been abolished and is frowned upon. Potential reasoning for this can be found in previous yugs where people may have had multiple partners because they could treat them equally and fairly; for example, in the story of the Ramayan, Maharaj Dasrath had three wives, Kaushalya, Sumitra and Kei Kei, who he treated all equally. As time has passed and we have emerged into different yugs, it would be increasingly difficult for us to provide equal love, care and affection to multiple partners. As a result, it would mean the individual would be committing a sin.

Some people may say God has created the concept of having many wives as some gods did have many wives.

However, what we must understand is things happen for a reason, and many times this is above our comprehension. We do not understand the fabrics of law and time. The example of Krishna Bhagwan having many wives will be illustrated here. Krishna Bhagwan had many gopis (wives), approximately 16,000. Krishna Bhagwan is an avatar of Vishnu Bhagwan. Vishnu Bhagwan had taken human birth previously in a different yug as Ram Bhagwan. Many men and women had confronted Ram Bhagwan and stated if they are reborn they would like to marry him in their next life. They all realised the true beauty of Ram Bhagwan and were in awe. They had seen his pure soul and godly qualities. Therefore, when Ram Bhagwan was born again on Earth as Krishna Bhagwan at a different time for a different need, all of the people who wished to marry Ram Bhagwan were able to marry Krishna Bhagwan. This is the reason behind the many gopis of Krishna Bhagwan.

One may ask whether a man can marry another man as Ram Bhagwan was approached by males; however, this is a concept that will not be understood by an individual who is not on the path of self-realisation. It was the soul of each man and woman within the human beings talking to Ram Bhagwan stating they wanted to marry him in their next life. The human body gives a gender to someone, but the soul has no gender. Therefore, it is perfectly acceptable for Ram Bhagwan to be approached in this manner.

In addition, Krishna Bhagwan's relationship with many gopis is not similar to a relationship we think of today. Their relationship would be one which is divine. There would be no physical contact, lustful desires, and jealousy involved in this. Just as importantly, who does not want a relationship with God? If many men loved Krishna Bhagwan and had a relationship with him, is this not the same thing? Everyone wants a relationship with God, but it's the new generation's understanding and thought process that does not understand the purity of the relationship with the many gopis.

How was forced marriage named a sin?

Forced marriages still occur in today's world despite it clearly being called a sin. Human beings' feeble minds are blindly following human made traditions as opposed to the important lessons taught by God. Krishna Bhagwan changed this tradition and deemed it to be morally wrong. Maharaj Bhishmaka (King Bhishmaka) was the ruler of Vidharba. He had a daughter named Rukmani. Rukmani's brother Rukmin was forcing her to marry Maharaj Shishupal (King Shishupal), the ruler of Chedi, an evil man who treated all in a poor manner. Ironically, Krishna Bhagwan and King Shishupal were cousins.

Rukmani, prior to the question of her marriage, already decided to deem Krishna Bhagwan as her husband. However, Rukmin opposed this idea and did not listen to Rukmani's wishes. Krishna Bhagwan came up with a plan to take Rukmani away and elope.

This highlights the significance of not forcing an individual to marry someone who they do not wish to.

In relation to this is a tradition of how parents choose their daughter's/son's partners, their daughters/sons having no choice in the matter. In reference to this, many parents force their child to marry a person of their choice instead of their child's. This is wrong and sinful. Krishna Bhagwan changed this tradition in the yug of the Mahabharat by portraying to the world that forced marriage was a sin through Rukmani's marriage dilemma; however, human nature—in particular their arrogance, pride and blindness—has meant they have not been able to convey this message.

Certain people want their child to marry only a certain type of caste so that they look good in front of others and can boast about how good their child is and what they have done. If the child wants to marry someone within their caste, then that is not a sin; however, if the child is being forced against their wishes to marry an individual for this reason, it is a sin.

The message of how a forced marriage is sinful was portrayed by Krishna Bhagwan in the Mahabharat. Duryodhan had come to Dwarka with a marriage proposal for Subhadra, Krishna Bhagwan's sister. Balram (Krishna Bhagwan's older brother) and Krishna Bhagwan had agreed for her to marry Duryodhan. After some time Krishna Bhagwan had noticed Subhadra was upset and had confronted her as to what was the matter. She told him that she had already accepted Arjun (one of the Panch Pandavs) to be her husband in her mind some time ago and now it has been agreed for her to marry Duryodhan. Krishna Bhagwan then asked Arjun to assist him and marry his sister to save her from misery.

Mahabharat was about change, changing the blindness of traditions that had caused pain, difficulty and unrighteousness to occur. As part of this change the tradition of parents/guardians choosing a partner for the child was changed. Krishna Bhagwan asked his sister what it was she wanted to do and who she wanted to marry. Despite this message, certain individuals cannot comprehend its meaning.

Is engaging in sexual activities with your partner a sin?

It is not sinful to engage in sexual activities with your partner during your life; however, as humans we must also attempt to control our minds. Some sadhus (saints) request to avoid engaging in sexual activities as it becomes very difficult for one to control their mind. The pleasure is like a drug and they need to do it, hence some people attempt to avoid engaging in sexual activities with their partners. Therefore, this informs us it is not a sinful act.

Another point to consider is there are other sadhus who state engaging in sexual activities for only pleasure is sinful and wrong and this should only be done if one wishes to reproduce. We shall look at an example to help understand this in more detail. When we consume food the primary reason to eat is to provide the body with nutrients, to be fit and healthy and exert energy to function. If we did not eat, we would eventually die. The secondary reason for consuming food is the taste. We eat certain types of foods due to the taste they have within them. In the same respect, the primary reason for engaging in sexual activities should be for reproduction and the secondary reason should be pleasure.

However, we do not have to go to these extremes. As stated previously, if we are not attached to engaging in sexual activities, it is fine. However, as soon as it becomes something you 'must do' you have become attached to the action, which is not good. This gives way to an individual not being able to control their mind and forgetting what their main aim in life is. A human being has the ability to think, create conscious thoughts and decide what action to take. We are the only living species on planet Earth who are able to do this. Therefore, we should use this knowledge and this ability to further ourselves. For example, if all an individual wanted to do was to engage in sexual activities, then what is the difference between them and an animal?

Chapter 8- Caste System

What is the caste system?

There are a few individuals who abide by the caste system (a system which details what job role a group of people will play in society) as law. However, there was no caste system thousands of years ago, meaning the caste system is man-made and not created by God.

When one sees a human being, they can identify if they are male or female. The question does not need to be asked: What gender are you? Whether someone is a male or female, the fact remains that they are a human being. In the same respect, all human beings should be viewed as the same and equal.

When an individual asks what caste you belong to, they are referring to something God did not create. God only created life, and as part of it humans were created. When creating humans, God created three common languages: laughter, crying and thoughts. All human beings cry and laugh in the same manner; it is a universal language. Even though not all humans think in the same way, we all have the ability to think and follow through a thought process, and this is also universal. All of the modern languages we speak today—English, German, French, Spanish, Hindi and so on—are all man made.

God did not scribe anywhere that these are the castes and these are the job roles each caste will carry out. Human beings would carry out a job and generally children would go into the line of work their father was in as this is what they knew. It would make it easy to work and earn a living. As a result of their jobs, many of their friends would be in the same line of work, for example farmers knew farmers, dentists knew dentists, grocery store owners knew other grocery store owners and so on. It got to a point where society started naming the groups of people working in a particular field. People who were farming were called farmers, people who repaired shoes were called mochi, people who repaired clothes were called darji, people who cut hair were called varand and so on. As a result of categorising these jobs, the caste system was created.

An individual's caste does not determine whether they are a good or bad human being. Someone could be a Brahmin (caste the sages and rishimunis belong to), but what does this truly mean? Does that mean they are automatically a good person? The answer is no, it does not. To determine an individual's values you must observe what they do with their Budhi (intellect), Tan (body), and Dhan (money – if they possess enough to help others). By analysing their actions considering these three attributes, you can understand whether that individual lives a dharmic life or not.

The caste system should not be used to differentiate people, discriminate against people and say you cannot do a certain activity because of your caste—this would be wrong. Nowhere in Hinduism does it state this, and this is one of the biggest misconceptions. For example, parents stating that their child must be married into the same caste as them are incorrect, and forcing them to marry into the same caste is also sinful. We are all made from the same 5 elements that each and every human being is made from, thus we are all a creation of God and all equal.

Many Hindus live by the caste system as a rule. This is not as common amongst younger, more modern Hindus; however, unfortunately, it does still exist. Let us take an example from a world-renowned book, *The End of History and the Last Man*. In this book there is a section which discusses religion and culture and the associated negative impacts on economic well-being. The religion that is used as an example that creates the greatest level of negative impact on economic well-being is Hinduism. The section reads, "There is a legion of cases where religion and culture have acted as obstacles. Hinduism, for example, is one of the few great world religions that is not based on a doctrine of the universal equality of man...Hindu doctrine divides human beings into complex series of castes that define their rights, privileges, and ways of life...it has seemingly constituted a barrier to economic growth".

In the Mahabharat there is an excellent example we can refer to. For reference of this example, the character of Karna shall be explained. Karna was the first son of Maharani Kunti (before she was married and became a queen). Maharani Kunti was the mother of the Panch Pandavs. In the early stages of her life she obtained a mantra (special prayer). This mantra was extremely powerful; when she recited the prayer and referred to a specific god, she would receive a child from that god as a blessing with their strengths. Being young and foolish, she had accidentally recited the prayer without realising that she invoked Surya Bhagwan (the sun god) to come forth and bless her with a child of his qualities. She could not give the child back as it was a blessing. Surya Bhagwan said she must keep him and said his son's name shall be Karna. Maharani Kunti informed her closest servant of what had happened and they both decided she could not keep the child as she was not married. If she had a child before marriage, no prince would marry her. It hurt her emotionally, but she felt as if there was no alternative choice at the time. She had put him into a basket and left him afloat in a river. Karna was found in a nearby village by Adhiratha and Radha, who took him in and raised him.

Adhiratha was the charioteer of Bhishma Pita. Nobody knew that this was Maharani Kunti's son, but everyone around Karna knew he was divine in quality and strength. He had a gold shield that appeared and disappeared on his body as and when he needed it. He was born with an impenetrable shield which formed part of his skin. He was also extremely strong and powerful.

During his childhood he felt a strong connection to warfare and wielding the bow in particular. He was extremely talented in using the bow; however, he and his father had many disagreements about using his bow in front of others as he was from the Sudh (a charioteer) caste. They drove the chariots of the army and king and never handled weapons; therefore, this was extremely looked down upon by his father. The king would forbid it, and if he found out he would be instructed to leave the city, as his caste was not assigned to do this job.

When the Panch Pandavs and the Kauravs returned from their many years of training with Guru Dronacharya, a large banquette and event was organised for each warrior to showcase their skills. There would be fights (with no killing) between each of the warriors to see who was the best. Arjun, one of the Panch Pandavs, specialised in wielding the bow and he won the competition with his excellent skill set. Guru Dronacharya claimed that Arjun was the best archer in the world, as that is how hard he trained him, and stated there was not anyone that could beat him. Not only had he mastered the art of warfare but also his senses.

Despite his father's many warnings, Karna jumped into the ring and confronted Arjun and challenged him to a duel. Guru Dronacharya asked who he was, and when Karna said he was a Sudh Putra (charioteer's son) and stated his father's name, Guru Dronacharya simply laughed and said, "What would you know about wielding a bow?" Bhishma Pita warned him to not do this and ordered him to leave the battle arena; however, Karna was determined to stay and fight. He argued that castes did not determine what skills and abilities an individual possessed. The crowd laughed at Karna and Bhishma Pita was getting frustrated. Karna's father was the charioteer of Bhishma Pita and ran onto the ground and asked for forgiveness.

Karna retaliated and opposed the apology and challenged Arjun. They started dueling and everything seemed equal. They were at that moment in time as good as each other. As they were dueling the sun had set. Dueling could not go beyond sunset as this would oppose the rules of warfare. There was no clear winner as no one lost, but they both agreed they would meet again and duel once more to determine who the best archer in the world was. They were in reality as good as each other.

At the end of the Mahabharat when Bhishma Pita was on his deathbed, he had asked for forgiveness from Karna for telling him that he could not wield a bow due to his caste. He realised towards the end of his life that it was a sin. Karna had forgiven him. These incidents happened thousands of years ago, and yet the same incidents happen in the world today in a different context. For example, there are many instances where individuals cannot marry into a different caste to their own. Have we not learnt from one of the greatest stories in history? If such a powerful, inspiring, pious man such as Bhishma Pita realised it was a sin and sought forgiveness, then should we not also realise it is wrong to discriminate due to an individual's caste?

Therefore understand your caste, be a part of your caste, but do not let this boost your ego and pride, and most certainly do not discriminate against someone due to their caste.

Chapter 9- Intoxications to the Body

Why is it that intoxications to the body are forbidden?

In the Vedic scriptures it states one should not intoxicate themselves.

Intoxications are to be avoided as it causes one to not be fully in control of their mind. We shall focus on the example of alcohol. Drinking alcohol is perceived as socially acceptable and is widespread. Individuals go for drinks for celebratory purposes, work drinks, social drinks to catch up with friends and family, and so on.

It does not explicitly state drinking is forbidden in Hinduism as it uses an umbrella term of intoxication. In fact drinking is not bad; the effect of drinking is what is bad. It is the way in which alcohol affects your behavior and state of mind that makes it bad. An extreme example is when one turns violent or is distraught. This change in an individual's state of mind can have negative effects and encourages actions which would result in bad karma. Remember our actions in the present pave the way for the immediate and long-term future.

However, alcohol can also change your state of mind subtly and affect your level of consciousness and your thoughts without you even realising. For example, after a few drinks you may behave differently to when you are sober. Think about it, do you actually act the same with alcohol in your system and without alcohol in your system? You may act in a more lustful manner, for example. This being said, the results can be detrimental as you are unable to control your mind in the same manner as you would without drinking alcohol.

There are very few people in this world that can control their state of mind regardless of what is happening or what they have taken. These individuals have a unique ability that is not present in common individuals. These abilities are a result of great taap (meditation) and possibly even karma from a previous life impacting them now.

If a person wishes to progress deeper into spiritual life, they will need to stop activities such as drinking in small quantities that pose a potential threat. As stated previously, it can also cause subtle changes in one's state of mind. Also as one does progress deeper into spiritual life, they will automatically want to reduce their involvement with activities such as this automatically. Their fascination and enjoyment for it shall disappear slowly and their interest in dharmic activities (righteous activities) shall increase.

This intellect applies to all intoxications across the board, including any sort of drug. It is vital to remember to keep your mind focused upon God as much as possible.

We must also remember that drugs do not simply relate to illegal classified drugs. For example, coffee and tea are classed as drugs. The effects of these drugs are not classed as detrimental, unlike alcohol or other drugs.

Intoxications of alcohol and drugs not only hamper our spiritual life but also our physical health. Intoxications can not only lead to addictions but also severe health problems. Alcohol and drug consumption can lead to liver, heart, brain, and bowel damage and much more. Furthermore, there are also mental health issues that can arise from this. Ultimately one has to be extremely careful when putting these substances into the body.

There are also other modern day intoxications that affect the body which are rarely spoken of. They could not be written about in scriptures by rishimunis as they did not exist then. However, all of the same principles taught by scriptures still apply to these modern day intoxications. The intoxication of television, magazines, newspapers, and social media can be just as damaging, if not worse than the intoxication of alcohol and drugs. There are things we see in all of these modern day intoxications which can have a bad effect on our minds. We want to be like all other rich and famous people we see and read about. We want all the new gadgets advertised, we want to have the perfect body like the models, we only want branded and expensive luxury goods, and so on.

These modern day intoxications implement materialistic desires in our minds which we do not necessarily need. We do not have to be extremely rich to enjoy our lives. Conversely, it is common for the rich to be dissatisfied or unhappy, and as a result need therapy. But then why are the poorest people happier? The answer to this is that they do not lose their moral values, they are grateful for what they have, and they do not need luxuries but simply the basics to survive. It is important to realise that materialistic objects are not essential in life and one muthe nest have the ability to live a simple life where they are able to survive with the necessities. The simpler you live your life, the happier you will be.

Television, social media and the news covertly dictate how we should act. Teenagers are exposed to television programmes where youths are drinking and partying in substantial amounts. What does this teach us? That acting in such a way is appropriate when in fact it is not. We begin to think behaving in this way on a regular basis is acceptable. Additionally, many music videos portray exposed women, large sums of money, alcohol and drugs as the prime content of the video. Again, what does this teach us?

This generation's youth and future generations will watch such videos and start believing that acting in such a way is acceptable as they do not know any better.

The news is informative but can be very prejudiced. News channels portray certain types of cultures and people in certain ways that can be very subjective. They pick out key descriptive words to do with one's race and culture to make a punchy article which all the viewers/readers hold on to. As a result, people will often assume that an individual will act or behave in a certain way due to their race, colour or culture. We need to remember that not everyone is the same and we must be compassionate and caring towards one another. The news will depict concepts in a certain way, predominantly for informative purposes but equally to evoke controversy or generate publicity.

Conclusively, we must not let modern day intoxications control us. We must use our mind and righteousness to understand how to act and behave and not be influenced by materialistic desires.

Chapter 10- Modern Day Issues

Is organ donation against principles of Hinduism?

It is widely believed in Hinduism that organ donation is forbidden. The rationale behind such a rule can be explained by the act of cremation. The cremation of the body signifies the soul 'burning' (i.e., destroying) the relationship formed to the body. This ensures the soul does not remain attached to the body and is able to move on to its future lifeform.

The rationale does seem logical; however, this is the thought of a very materialistic and worldly view. Let us think about this. How do we identify when an individual has passed away? We identify this by acknowledging the individual is no longer breathing and as a result their heart has stopped beating. In the same respect when an individual stops breathing (i.e., passes away) the soul leaves the body.

The soul will progress into moksh or future life forms regardless of whether the body it resided in is cremated or not. The only situation where the soul will not progress into moksh or future lifeforms is if there was a deeply rooted desire the soul wished to complete and it was not able to fulfil that desire. This is where the soul remains on Earth, which is most commonly known as bhooth (ghost). The occurrence of the soul remaining on earth is irrelevant to whether the body is cremated or not.

Once an individual has passed away, the body they once occupied is of no use to them anymore; therefore, why not let it be of use to another individual?

Apart from this myth, there are other reasons such as personal preference and family members who do not wish this to happen as the organs may be removed before they see the individual after they have passed away. However, apart from this, the traditional view of organ donation being forbidden in Hinduism is no longer relevant as explained above.

In fact, this sort of practice should be promoted, not discouraged. After all we are providing individuals with a chance at life, what greater satisfaction could there be?

The only aspect we must consider is our organs may be donated to individuals who may commit great atrocities or sinful actions using the organs. In such a case the organ donor would also be part responsible from a karmic perspective and would receive bad karma. However, how can an organ donor know what an individual will be like after their passing? The answer is they do not. As a result, the organ donor does what is right by them and attempts to help someone in need. What happens after that is something they cannot control.

Is adoption and IVF against the principles of Hinduism?

Unfortunately in life some couples are unable to reproduce naturally. The question then arises: Can one use IVF or adoption as an alternative?

IVF is an acronym for 'In Vitro Fertilisation'. IVF is the process whereby eggs are collected from either the hopeful mother or sperm is collected from the hopeful father/donor or both. Medication is used to boost the number of eggs produced. The eggs from the hopeful mother/donor and sperm from the hopeful father/donor are mixed in the hope the egg will become fertilised. Once the egg is fertilised, it becomes an embryo (the starting of a human baby being formed). The embryo is then placed into a surrogate mother's womb (woman who will carry the embryo) where the embryo will hopefully grow into a foetus (a human baby when inside a mother). IVF is unsuccessful in many cases, but in the cases where it does work it is a dream come true for the future parents of the child to be born.

One may ask, is it right for humankind to abuse science in this manner? Are humans acting like God? The answer is it is not incorrect for such treatments to be implemented in this way. We are intelligent beings using the power God has granted us with. Ultimately, the treatment is used to provide hopeful couples or individuals with a fighting chance to become parents. This act is not harming anyone or anything in the process; therefore, it is not morally wrong.

In reality if a couple were destined not to bear children due to their karma, no matter what treatment they tried they would not be able to become parents. But how do people know if they are not destined to be parents if they do not try the remedies available to them?

Adoption is also an alternative. Adoption is the act of taking on the legal responsibilities of a child that is not one's biological child.

To clarify, this is not forbidden in Hinduism and is not morally or spiritually incorrect. In fact, individuals are reluctant to choose this option and the main reason for this is the child is not of their own flesh and blood. There is no wrong or right answer to this as it is the personal preference of the couple who face the issue of not being able to conceive.

Furthermore, another point of common concern is in relation to the child's upbringing. There have been such cases where couples have adopted a child, and due to the upbringing of the child (prior to adoption) they have badly mistreated, stolen from or killed their foster parents. However, we cannot think of this solely from a negative point of view.

There are, of course, positives as well. There also have been cases where the adopted child has made the foster parents happier than their own flesh and blood and done more for the foster parents than their own families have done.

Furthermore, the act of adoption is a great act indeed. It is providing a child with love, care and a chance for a better life.

Ultimately, as stated above, this is a personal choice and there is no right or wrong answer, but to conclude this is not religiously incorrect from a Hinduism, moral or spirituality perspective.

A thought to leave you with...

A human being is not bound by their deeds but the expectations expected from these deeds. For example, if you expect to receive good fortune from donating a large sum of money and this does not occur, you may carry out an action in retaliation to that. This act/feeling will bind you to another result and potential rebirth. However, if you do receive good fortune, you may become reliant upon constant good fortune every time you carry out a charitable act, thus increasing your ignorance and making you blind as to the purpose of donating.

It is crucial to keep happiness and sadness as equals without thinking about gain, loss, victory, or defeat and carrying out your duty to live a righteous life. In this manner you will not obtain sin. This is called karma yoga.

One who has understood sankya yog understands they are not the body but merely a soul, and a human life is merely an illusion. This person will find it easier to carry out karma yoga.

One may question the world and their purpose. If this is all an illusion, they may opt to live in solitude and concentrate their efforts on God. However, it is the opposite of this that needs to be done. If those who understand duty and righteousness leave, who will then be the leaders of society? This leaves a chance for unrighteous individuals to rule society. For example, in the Mahabharat, if Bhishma Pita did not renounce the world by opting for sanyas (a life of celibacy which is dedicated to God), unrighteousness would not have grown so much.

A karma yogi stays in this world like a saint. They perform all actions but do not lose themselves in these actions, i.e. they do not become attached to normal daily life actions. A karma yogi does not expect anything from anyone, including loved ones, and they themselves reap the benefits of sanyas by not having expectations.

You must let go of all your bad habits, misdeeds and poor traits, thereby freeing yourself from the shackles of sin. From letting go you can begin a life full of bliss and remembrance of God.

We must consider all of our cravings and abolish the need for them. We must not be attached to them. One whose mind does not waver after failure and keeps strong and one who does not become egotistic after success has the traits of a karma yogi. Such a person succeeds in all aspects of life repeatedly.

In order to keep a strong mind and not expect outcomes from deeds, one must remember God. It will be beneficial to them. It gives rise to a feeling of submission, which in reality is called devotion. Devotion will enlighten a human being and help them differentiate between right and wrong, and consequently they can catch a glimpse of the Almighty. To catch a glimpse of God, remove the bandage from your eyes that consists of greed, pride, anger and prejudice. How can a blind man in a dark room worship the sun? If the blind man comes out into the open under the sky, the sun is already present. In the same respect, the entire universe is made up of God. One who sees his soul can see God.

One who catches a glimpse of the Almighty truly becomes the most dutiful. He is freed from the circle of birth and rebirth and attains moksh.

Glossary

100 Kauravs – The 100 Kauravs were the 100 sons of King Dhitrasth and Queen Gandhari. The epic tale of Mahabharat revolved around these characters as they fought for unrighteousness

Ahimsa – Law of non-violence

Arjun – One of the Panch Pandavs who was renowned for his archery skills and was one of the main characters in the epic tale of the Mahabharat.

BAPS Swaminarayan Sanstha – A sect (a branch) of Hinduism founded by Bhagwan Swaminarayan (1781-1830). It was formally established in 1907 by Shastriji Maharaj (1865-1951)

BCE – Before the Common Era (use of dates before the Christian era, i.e. before Jesus Christ was born)

Bhagwan Parshuram – An avatar of Lord Vishnu born in the Treta Yug to kill evil Kshatriya's (warriors) doing unjust in the world

Bhagvat Gita – One of Hinduisms most famous and commonly referred to religious scripture. Bhagvat Gita details Krishna Bhagwan's life and the epic story of the Mahabharat

Brahma Bhagwan – This translates to God Brahmna (also referred to as Lord Brahma and many other names). Lord Brahma is one of the Tri-Murti Gods (3 Supreme Gods). Lord Brahma is the Lord of Creation

Brahma Kumaris – A spiritual organisation which started in 1937

Caste System – A system of categorising people into what job functions they would carry out many years ago

Chakra – Translates into wheel/disk which is required to help the body function. There are seven chakras in total. The first one is near the bladder and the seventh one (the highest level which allows you to reach self-realisation) is at the top of your head

Demigod – A god of lower divine status than the Tri-Murti gods

Dharma – Law and code of conduct which teaches an individual how to life an ideal life

Dwarka – The kingdom of Lord Krishna found in Gujarat, India

Ekadashi – 11th day of each half month in the Vedic lunar calendar where fasting is observed for Lord Krishna

Ganpati Bapa – This translates to Ganpati Grandfather. This is Lord Shiva's son, also known as Lord Ganesh. Lord Ganesh is an omen of good fortune and looks after all of creation—hence the name Ganpati Bapa. Like an older family member, he looks after everyone. Lord Ganesh is famously known for his elephant head

Guru – A guru is defined as a teacher. This can be anyone who teaches you something and is not reflective of only formal education

Guru Purnima – A special day observed on the full moon day during Ashadha month (June-July) as per the Hindu calendar. This day is where students pay their respect to their gurus and thank them for their teachings.

Gunas – Three qualities of nature (prakriti), which are inaction despite having knowledge (Rajas), carrying out actions only for personal pleasure (Tamas), and goodness or purity (Sattva)

Hanuman Bhagwan – This translates to God Hanuman (also referred to as Lord Hanuman and many other names). Hanuman Bhagwan is the son of King Kesari and Queen Anjani and is a form of Shankar Bhagwan. He had taken part in the great Ramayan battle.

Hare Krishna – A sect of Hinduism created in 1965 by A.C. Bhaktivedanta Swami Prabhupada worshipping Lord Krishna

Jainism – Jainism is a world religion which emphasises non-violence and spirituality with the aim of liberation from the cycle of birth and death

Karma – Law of cause and effect. Each action has a result which the actionee must bear

Karma Yoga – The art of not expecting an outcome from an action and therefore not causing a resultant karma, forcing attachment or re-birth in another life

Krishna Bhagwan – This translates to God Krishna (also referred to as Lord Krishna and many other names). Krishna Bhagwan was a re-incarnation of Lord Vishnu, who had taken birth in Dwapar Yug to eliminate evil on the earth. He had taken part in the great Mahabharat battle

Kriyaman Karma – Karma where the fruit of the action is received instantly

Kuruksetra – The battleground found in Hastinapur where the epic tale of Mahabharat took place (modern day New Delhi)

Kshatriya – A warrior caste (group of people) in India. The job role of people born in this caste was to join and serve their respective king's army

Kurdevi – Families worship a particular goddess who they call their Kurdevi. They have a special connection with this goddess as generations of their family have prayed to the same goddess for the family's welfare

Mahabharat – Mahabharat is an epic tale detailing a holy war that occurred between the Pandavs and the Kauravs

Mandir – A place of worship for Hindus

Murti – A statue of God used for worship

Nishkam Bhakti – Carrying out Dharma but not getting attached to the outcome of our actions, i.e. we don't expect something positive in return

Panch Pandavs – The five sons of Queen Kunti: Yudishtr, Bheem, Arjun, Nakul and Sahadev. The epic tale of the Mahabharat revolved around these characters as they fought for righteousness

Paramatma – The supreme and omnipresent God that is in all of creation

Parsotam Mayno – The lunar calendar adds one extra month every third year, which is called Parsotam Mayno. Charitable acts and fasting are believed to be very fruitful during this time

Prabhada Karma – Karma that has ripened and the fruit of the action can be received

Prapti – Something which is eternal

Ram Bhagwan - This translates to God Ram (also referred to as Lord Ram and many other names). Ram Bhagwan was a re-incarnation of Lord Vishnu who had taken birth in Treta Yug to eliminate evil on the Earth. He had taken part in the great Ramayan battle

Ramcharitmanas – Literature written by Tulsidas about the life of Ram Bhagwan

Ravan – Ravan was the unrighteous demon that Ram Bhagwan was born to kill in the epic tale of Ramayan. He was incredibly powerful, knowledgeable and used to be a devotee of Shankar Bhagwan

Rig Veda – One of the four books which codified the ideas and practices of the Vedic religion and laid down the basis of classical Hinduism. They were probably composed between 1500 and 700 BC and contain hymns, philosophy, and guidance on ritual

Righteousness – Being truthful, honest and acting in the appropriate manner Dharma teaches

Rishimuni – An ordained priest who has the ability to carry out yagnas

Sadhu – An individual who has left normal life, detached themselves from the world and materialistic desires to lead a simple life to find/be one with God. The aim is to become spiritually enlightened and self-realised (also known as a sanyasi)

Sanathan Dharma – Origins of modern day Hinduism meaning eternal way/eternal truth

Sanchit Karma – Karma that is stored in a pool where it awaits to be ripened to provide the prescribed result of the action at the destined time

Sankya Yog – The science behind the soul and the body being two different aspects

Sanyasi – An individual who has left normal life, detached themselves from the world and materialistic desires to lead a simple life to find/be one with God. The aim is to become spiritually enlightened and self-realised (also known as a sadhu)

Sat Guru – The ultimate guru (teacher) who shows you the path of enlightenment, i.e. what life is truly about

Shankar Bhagwan – This translates to God Shankar (also referred to as Lord Shiva and many other names). Shankar Bhagwan is one of the Tri-Murti Gods (3 Supreme Gods). Shankar Bhagwan is the Lord of Destruction (death)

Shastra – Sanskrit term meaning code, rules, or treatise in Vedic scriptures

Shishya – A pupil of a teacher

Shivling – A symbol which identifies the places where Lord Shiva had visited/resided

Shravan Mayno – A holy month that normally falls in August. The story details it is the month where the churning of the ocean took place and a poison was released. This was consumed by Lord Shiva and preserved in his throat, turning it blue. Hence he is also known as Neelkanth (blue throated one)

Shrimad Bhagvatam – A religious scripture consisting of a collection of stories regarding Lord Vishnu by which important lessons of Hinduism are taught

Sita Mata (Sitaji) – This translates to Mother Sita (also referred to as Goddess Sita and many other names). Sitaji was a re-incarnation of Goddess Swaraswati (Vishnu Bhagwan's wife) who had taken birth in Treta Yug to eliminate evil on the Earth. She was the wife of Ram Bhagwan and had a pivotal role in the great Ramayan story

Soul – The energy with our bodies that allows the body to function

Upanishads – Various holy scriptures that form the core of Indian philosophy that helped formulate the Vedic scriptures. The Upanishads discuss self-realisation, yoga and meditation

Vedas – Four books: Rig Veda – the most important and, according to scholars, oldest of the Vedas; Yajur Veda –

details the performance of yagnas (ceremonies); Sama Veda– chants and melodies to be sung during worship and the performance of yagnas; and Atharva Veda – contains hymns, mantras and incantations for outside of yagnas. These 4 books codified the ideas and practices of the Vedic religion and laid down the basis of classical Hinduism. They were probably composed between 1500 and 700 BC

Vishnu Bhagwan – This translates to God Vishnu (also referred to as Lord Vishnu and many other names). Vishnu Bhagwan is one of the Tri-Murti Gods (3 Supreme Gods). Vishnu Bhagwan is the Lord of Preservation. He takes various avatars (re-incarnations) through the ages to restore righteousness, justice and truth

Yagna – Holy rituals led by priests for various reasons. This usually involves fire (seen as sacred and holy) and offerings such as flowers, ghee (purified butter) and sesame seeds

Yug – Refers to the ages of time in the world. There are 4 Yugs: Satya Yug, Treta Yug, Dwapar Yug and Kali Yug

References

- Albert Einstein. 2012. Albert Einstein. [ONLINE] Available at: http://einstein.biz/biography.php. [Accessed 05 July 15].
- BBC. 2014. BBC. [ONLINE] Available at: http://www.bbc.co.uk/news/health-28797106. [Accessed 05 July 15].
- BBC Bite Size. 2011. BBC Bite Size. [ONLINE] Available at: http://www.bbc.co.uk/schools/gcsebitesize/science/21c/life_on_earth/species_interdependencerev4.shtml. [Accessed 05 July 15].
- Bharat Swabhiman. (2012). Completely cure Cancer Though Pranayam -IIT khadakpur Student. [Online Video]. 26 November. Available from: https://www.youtube.com/watch?v=A3LWYV7C7XI&app=desktop. [Accessed: 05 July 2015].
- Biography. 2015. Biography. [ONLINE] Available at: http://www.biography.com/people/mahatma-gandhi-9305898#spiritual-and-political-leader. [Accessed 05 July 15].
- Bodhasarananda. Swami. 1947. Powers of the Mind
- Cancer Research. 2015. Cancer Research. [ONLINE] Available at: http://www.cancerresearchuk.org/about-

cancer/cancers-in-general/treatment/complementary-alternative/therapies/yoga. [Accessed 05 July 15].

- ebusinessmantra. 2015. VivekAnanda Vedanta Network. [ONLINE] Available at: http://vivekananda.org/biography.asp. [Accessed 05 July 15].

- Facebook. Baba Ramdev. [ONLINE] Available at: https://www.facebook.com/swami.ramdev/info?tab=page_info. [Accessed 05 July 15].

- Fisher, J. 1993. The Case for Reincarnation. London: Diamond Books

- Head, J. and Cranston, S. 1970. Reincarnation- An East-West Anthology. Wheaton: The Theosophical Publishing House

- Heart of Hinduism. 2004. Heart of Hinduism. [ONLINE] Available at: http://hinduism.iskcon.org/concepts/108.htm. [Accessed 05 July 15].

- Human Kinetics. Human Kinetics. [ONLINE] Available at: http://www.humankinetics.com/excerpts/excerpts/how-our-bodies-use-protein. [Accessed 05 July 15].

- Jehovah's witnesses. 2015. How Did Life Begin

- Maldev Bapa, Lecture on Hinduism Questions, April 2014-July 2015

- Mukundcharandas, Sadhu. 2012. Karma and Reincarnation in Hinduism

- Scienceaid.co.uk. 2012. Scienceaid.co.uk. [ONLINE] Available at: http://scienceaid.co.uk/biology/ecology/food.html. [Accessed 05 July 15].

- Stevenson. I. 1997. Reincarnation and Biology. Vol II: Birth defects and other anomalies. West Port: Praeger

- Swami Jnaneshvara Bharati. 2004. Yoga Meditation Index. [ONLINE] Available at: http://www.swamij.com/index-yoga-meditation-about.htm. [Accessed 05 July 15].

- The Guardian. 2014. The Guardian. [ONLINE] Available at: http://www.theguardian.com/science/2014/mar/04/animal-protein-diets-smoking-meat-eggs-dairy. [Accessed 05 July 15].

Made in the USA
Charleston, SC
11 November 2016